Middle Grades
Social Studies

Related Titles of Interest

Teaching and Learning Elementary Social Studies, 6/e
Arthur K. Ellis
ISBN: 0-205-26763-7

The Collaborative Social Studies Classroom: A Resource for Teachers, Grades 7-12
Joseph John Nowicki and Kerry F. Meehan
ISBN: 0-205-17391-8

Literature-Based History Activities for Children, Grades 4-8
Patricia L. Roberts
ISBN: 0-205-14737-2

Classroom-Ready Activities for Teaching History and Geography in Grades 7-12
Thomas P. Ruff and Jennifer T. Nelson
ISBN: 0-205-26375-5

For more information or to purchase a book, please call 1-800-278-3525.

SECOND EDITION

MIDDLE GRADES SOCIAL STUDIES

Teaching and Learning for Active
and Responsible Citizenship

MICHAEL G. ALLEN

Georgia Southern University

ROBERT L. STEVENS

Georgia Southern University

Allyn and Bacon

Boston • London • Toronto • Sydney • Tokyo • Singapore

Series Editor: Frances Helland
Series Editorial Assistant: Kris Lamarre
Marketing Manager: Kathy Hunter
Advertising Manager: Anne Morrison
Manufacturing Buyer: Suzanne Lareau

Copyright © 1998, 1994 by Allyn & Bacon
A Viacom Company
Needham Heights, MA 02194

Internet: www.abacon.com
America Online: keyword: College Online

Library of Congress Cataloging-in-Publication Data

Allen, Michael G.
    Middle grades social studies : teaching and learning for active
and responsible citizenship / Michael G. Allen, Robert L. Stevens. —
2nd ed.
        p. cm.
    Includes bibliographical references and index.
    ISBN 0-205-27118-9
    1. Social sciences-Study and teaching (Secondary)-United States.
I. Stevens, Robert L.   II. Title.
H62.5U5a448 1998   97-15612
300'.71'273-dc21   CIP

Printed in the United States of America
10 9 8 7 6 5 4 3 2   01 00 99

To Robert V. Supple, teacher, mentor, friend,
and comrade in the struggle to improve social studies
for young Americans. Although distance and disease
prevented a final time of sharing and caring,
our correspondence made a difference and, though you
did not know of this dedication before you left us,
this one is for you, Bob.

Michael G. Allen

To the memory of Grace Agustas Lord Leach,
my great-grandmother, whose love of history and
interest in her community, Portsmouth, New
Hampshire, has left a lasting influence. She always
said, "Those who are fortunate to be intelligent and
healthy have an obligation to participate in their
community for its continuation and improvement."

Robert L. Stevens

CONTENTS

PREFACE

In the preface to our first edition, we reflected on the 1980s as a decade of turmoil and trouble. As we near the beginning of the twenty-first century, our assessment has not changed. The United States has been at war in the Middle East and at this writing appears on the brink of another conflict in the same region. Consumer debt is at an all-time high. Drug use is, once again, front-page news as statistics point to a dramatic increase in the use of illegal drugs and alcohol by young and old alike.

In reflecting on these and related changes into the decade of the 1990s and beyond, we believe social studies continues to play a pivotal role in the development of attitudes and values that not only promote active and responsible citizenship among school-age youngsters, but also offer real hope in facing and overcoming some of the serious problems challenging people throughout the nation and beyond.

Social studies relishes the mandate to prepare young people for active and responsible citizenship in our constitutional democracy. In the short term, social studies must continue to address mandates for more content—social science concepts and generalizations, multicultural education, global education, law-related education, humanities, U.S. and non-Western history, and geography. It must teach skills for acquiring, organizing, and using information, and for fostering and improving interpersonal relationships. Educators must also encourage participation in the actions of the body politic and ensure the development of a truly functional set of democratic values and beliefs. In the long term, these same educators must prepare youngsters to confront and solve seemingly intractable problems and address ethical issues and matters of public policy unheard of a decade ago.

During early adolescence, social studies comes into its own as a discrete entity in the school curriculum. But even in the middle grades, despite a developing focus on a more integrated approach to curriculum and learning, social studies remains a stepchild to the three R's, a fragmented effort to inform students. Early adolescents are at a unique developmental stage, when we must impress on them the necessity for active and responsible citizenship, as well as an appreciation for social studies content and skills in achieving such a level of citizenship.

Middle Grades Social Studies offers preservice and practicing middle grades educators the following: (1) an overview of the historical and philosophical antecedents of social studies education; (2) a brief review of the developmental characteristics of early adolescence; (3) concrete examples of programs designed to engage students in developing the knowledge and skills for active and responsible citizenship; and (4) a range of tested ideas for challenging young adolescents with academic experiences that address their unique developmental profile and capture their imaginations. Further, this book is designed to help social studies teachers become key players in the current movement toward more interdisciplinary-integrated curriculum and instruction.

In addition to a general updating and revision of this second edition, Chapters 4, 5, and 6 have been significantly revised. The section on CAAP has been considerably shortened, and information on service learning has been added, with a concrete example of an ongoing and successful service-learning project. Further, we focus on the new national standards for the social studies as well as the volatile issue of public values and character education. With the addition of a number of new and revised critical thinking activities, all the activities have been organized into a lesson plan format to make it easier for students and teachers either to use them directly or to adapt them to their respective classrooms. We believe these revisions render the text more clearly classroom specific and user-friendly.

Although it is impossible to consider every segment of social studies education in a single book, this book should serve methods courses in general and as a basic text for middle grades social studies methods courses in particular.

We would like to thank the following reviewers who helped guide us with thoughtful ideas during this revision: Robert L. Gilstrap, George Mason University; Jesus Garcia, University of Illinois.

PART I

THEORY

CHAPTER 1
Reviewing the Past, Assessing the Present, Looking to the Future

CHAPTER 2
The Nature of Social Studies

CHAPTER 3
Early Adolescence: A Time of Change and Transition

In Part I, we challenge the reader to consider carefully the current state of social studies education in the middle schools of the United States. We focus on the role of the teacher, use of the textbook, modes of instruction, motivation, social studies content, and affective components of the social studies curriculum. Clearly, the problems facing social studies teachers mirror the problems and challenges in the wider society.

In Chapter 1, the reader is introduced to several conclusions and recommendations related to the state of social studies education in the United States. These are based on an analysis of the field and are related specifically to middle grades education. Categories about which our conclusions are drawn include: textbooks, curriculum, instruction, knowledge, motivation, affective education, controversial issues, student apathy, skill development, early adolescent development, student personal development, becoming an active professional, and the middle school movement.

In Chapter 2, we focus on the nature of social studies through an analysis of four traditions extant in the field—social studies taught as citizenship transmission, as social science, as reflective inquiry, and as personal development. We discuss each tradition within the framework of its purpose, method, and content. We define and discuss social studies and the related objectives necessary to implement a successful social studies program.

Each objective of social studies—knowledge, skills, values, and participation—is described and discussed at length, with direct connections made to sound middle grades education. We also offer practical application of each objective and its components to sound practice in middle grades social studies.

Finally, in Chapter 3 we focus on the developmental characteristics of early adolescents. This discussion revolves around the broad categories of physical, social, emotional, and intellectual developmental characteristics.

Before approaching practice components in Part II, the reader is urged to build a firm understanding of the various theoretical perspectives of social studies education, sound middle-level education, and the characteristics of early adolescent development. Such an understanding will broaden his or her views as to the importance of a more integrated focus in middle grades social studies.

1

REVIEWING THE PAST, ASSESSING THE PRESENT, LOOKING TO THE FUTURE

The classroom teacher is the most powerful force shaping social studies goals and objectives. The teacher's beliefs, social studies knowledge base, and understanding of early adolescents and the learning resources available mold the nature of any social studies program.

Teachers may have little control over budget and only occasional influence on the selection of textbooks, but they are the final arbiters of what occurs in their classrooms. Any curricular change that is not viewed favorably by teachers can be effectively vetoed. Recognizing that any change or improvement in social studies lies largely in the hands of teachers, this chapter is designed to challenge readers with a series of conclusions and recommendations that relate directly to middle grades social studies.

The broad goals of middle grades education are to complement more specific social studies goals and should take into consideration the general needs and expectations of students. Specifically, according to Alexander (1988), every middle school student

1. Should be well-known as a person by at least one adult in the school who accepts responsibility for the student's guidance.
2. Should be helped to achieve optimum mastery of the skills or continued learning together with a commitment to their use and improvement.
3. Should have ample experiences designed to develop decision-making and problem-solving skills.

4. Should acquire a functional body of fundamental knowledge.
5. Should have opportunities to explore and develop interests in aesthetic, leisure, career, and other aspects of life.

Any changes made in social studies programming should take these five general perspectives into account. General program goals in social studies should also complement more specific expectations. For example, middle-level social studies programs ought to develop functional knowledge, skills, values, and personal or social behavior repertoires that empower early adolescents to

1. Consider intelligently the complex issues that affect daily living in our society.
2. Formulate value/moral systems that promote responsible and thoughtful responses to personal and social issues.
3. Develop a sense of "enoughness" in the context of personal lifestyle and standard of living.
4. Develop a sense of global interdependence.
5. Develop skills and predispositions associated with democratic living.
6. Formulate visions of the future toward which personal and social action may be directed. (Toepfer, 1988, p. 112)

CURRENT REALITIES

While exemplary social studies programs exist and many educators are doing an excellent job of teaching, research findings make it clear that reform is still needed. In spite of a growing number of middle grades schools that exemplify the best characteristics of sound middle school education (Alexander & McEwin, 1989), there remain others that need basic improvements in both curriculum and programs.

This section draws extensively on the findings of three national studies sponsored by the National Science Foundation (Stake & Easley, 1978; Weiss, 1978; Wiley, 1977) and reported by Shaver, Davis, and Helburn (1979). These studies offer insight into the nature of classroom practices and confirm the continuing view that social studies instruction has changed little since the 1920s, even in middle grades schools where some of the most innovative and far-reaching changes have occurred in the 1970s and 1980s. Recent shadow study research also supports these findings, especially for middle schools.

The major conclusions from these studies (Shaver et al., 1979) include the following:

1. Teachers are the key to what social studies will be for any student, and they have the power to render ineffective any curricular change not meeting their approval.
2. Materials from the federally funded social studies projects of the 1960s and 1970s are not being selected for classroom use.
3. The dominant instructional tool continues to be the conventional textbook, and long-time best-sellers continue to dominate the market.
4. The curriculum focuses mostly on history and government, with geography included at the elementary and middle/junior high school levels. There is little interdisciplinary teaching and little attention paid to social issues.
5. The dominant mode of instruction continues to be large-group, teacher-controlled recitation and lecture, based primarily on the textbook.
6. The "knowing" expected of students is largely information-oriented. Students often have to reproduce the content and language of the book. Experience-based curricula and inquiry teaching are rare.
7. Teachers rely on external motivation. Students are not expected to learn because of their own interest, but because completion of the lessons usually means achieving better grades.
8. Students generally find social studies content and modes of instruction uninteresting.
9. Affective objectives are rarely an explicit part of the curriculum. Implicitly, content and classroom considerations are used to teach students to accept authority and to imbibe "important truths" uncritically.

When the unique nature of early adolescence is considered in relation to such findings, it is evident that improvement and reorientation are needed in middle grades social studies. Clearly, the initiative for improvement must emanate from individual teachers if it is to prove effective.

In the spirit of great expectation, we offer a series of conclusions and recommendations for restructuring middle-level social studies education. They are designed not only to challenge your thinking but also to offer a range of possibilities for change and redirection.

CONCLUSIONS AND RECOMMENDATIONS

Textbooks

Most social studies instruction is limited to the use of the standard textbook, on which most teachers rely almost exclusively. Although a number of teachers complain about the use of textbooks as the primary instructional tool, many find them appropriate and adequate for virtually all instruction.

The standard social studies textbook, when used as a major resource for instruction, has much to commend it. Carefully selected, it is probably the single most important source for basic social studies curriculum and related instructional practices. The problem arises when it is used by teachers as the primary source of academic content. When the textbook is viewed as the principal authoritative source, the kind of interactive, hands-on instruction that is most effective with early adolescents is difficult to achieve.

Exclusive use of the social studies textbook in unimaginative ways discourages students from thinking about a multitude of important issues currently challenging the United States. Overuse or misuse of textbooks retards the development of reflective thinkers who wish to participate in and influence society through active involvement. The textbook should be used in ways that allow early adolescents to learn more than memorized facts. Limiting knowledge to this degree often produces passive, uninvolved citizens who have little understanding of social studies goals or of how to develop a commitment to active and responsible citizenship.

Therefore, it is necessary not only to carefully select social studies textbooks, but to also use a wide variety of supplemental resources. It is also important to point out to students the textbook's limitations as well as its benefits.

Curriculum

The middle grades social studies curriculum is largely limited to history, government, and geography, with little interdisciplinary teaching occurring.

Social studies should not be taught in isolated segments. A wider, more integrated experience is more appropriate and leads to a deeper understanding of life's complexities. As important as history, government, and geography are as separate fields of study, they are best taught from an interdisciplinary perspective (Alexander & George, 1981, 1993; Beane, 1990; Stevenson, 1992; Vars, 1987). Such an interdisciplinary, integrated mix ought to incorporate information from the social sciences, humanities, and personal life experiences of students within the core curriculum.

Early adolescents are moving into a developmental stage at which they are able to understand interrelationships (Lewbel, 1989). When presented on their intellectual level, interrelationships may be understood for the first time. However, when instruction is limited to highly structured classes with little integration of subject matter and personal experiences, meaningful learning is severely limited, and motivation is usually low.

Although middle grades social studies should emphasize history, government, and geography (*Expectations of Excellence*, 1994; *Geography for Life*, 1994), numerous opportunities for integrating other social science disciplines and the humanities should be presented in an interdisciplinary and integrated manner. Both interdisciplinary and integrated units should be utilized with continuous team-based planning among social studies teachers and their colleagues in other subject areas.

Instruction

The dominant modes of instruction continue to be large-group, teacher-dominated, and teacher-controlled recitation and lecture based primarily on the textbook. An examination of the developmental characteristics of early adolescence makes it clear that instruction limited to recitation and lecture will not be highly successful (Lounsbury & Johnston, 1988). Social studies content has unsurpassed potential when many exciting and interesting learning experiences are integrated into the ongoing curriculum.

Methods and activities appropriate for students include simulation games; audiovisual materials; bulletin boards; independent and small group projects; guest speakers; open and guided discussions; value-clarifying activities; learning activity packages; exchange programs; pen pals; festivals of various countries and communities; case studies; speaking opportunities; field trips; and community and social action projects and service learning projects. A wide variety of teaching methods and materials should be used in middle grades social studies instruction.

Knowing

The "knowing" expected of students is largely information-oriented, with students often not only having to repeat on tests and in discussions the content of the textbook, but also often having to use the language of the textbook.

This finding is a sad commentary on social studies instruction. Fortunately, there are numerous middle grades teachers who do not fit this category! As noted by Shaver et al. (1979), students are generally "expected to learn and respect understandings that come from others, assumedly validated, but by processes that are not explicated, much less brought up during classroom discourse to be examined and applied by students" (p. 151).

The "knowing" expected of students should not be limited to information to be repeated but should reflect a wide variety of learning strategies and teaching and learning styles (Stevens, 1990). Information in the social studies textbook should be examined critically, discussed, and connected to past and current realities. Experience-based curricula, such as community and social action projects, and service-learning projects, may be incorporated into all middle grades social studies programs.

Motivation

Teachers tend to rely on external motivation, and students generally find social studies content and modes of instruction uninteresting. Given the focus on textbooks and the reliance on external motivation, it is not surprising that students find social studies boring.

Early adolescents are at a stage at which challenging social studies experiences could be powerful motivators for important social learning, as well as for attitude and value development. However, radical approaches to teaching and learning are not required. Rather, the use of challenging, action-oriented, interdisciplinary, and integrated curriculum and instructional activities are easily incorporated into any existing social studies program.

It is an accepted principle of learning that knowledge gained by persons interested and involved in the process is retained longer and proves more meaningful. This alone is sufficient reason to focus on improving middle grades social studies programming. Most early adolescents are insufficiently mature to conceptualize the importance of learning how to better themselves in the future. They are primarily present-oriented and learn more readily when internally motivated.

Classroom learning should be organized in ways that recognize that both internal and external motivation are important to promoting active involvement in social studies.

Affective Education

Affective objectives are rarely an explicit part of the social studies curriculum. Unfortunately, "content and classroom interactions are typically used to teach students to accept authority and to have them learn 'important truths' about our history and government" (Shaver et al., 1979).

Attitudes and values are formed and solidified during early adolescence. This reality holds many implications for social studies instruction, including the need to address, rather than avoid, value-laden and controversial issues.

The flexibility of values during this developmental period carries with it both heavy responsibilities and exciting opportunities on the part of social studies instructors. Social studies is rich with opportunities for value development, as early adolescents begin for the first time to gain a more realistic understanding of such emotions as love and hate, to question the rationalizations given for war and social injustices, and other types of overt and covert human behavior. This time is also described as the "last best chance" for early adolescents to learn those attitudes, values, and behaviors that will serve them best in adulthood (Carnegie Council, 1989).

It is an opportune time to assist these youths in obtaining a broader understanding of critical value-related issues. Exposure to value conflicts through literature, films, community involvement, and other activities provides an excellent forum for dealing with developing adultlike emotions and beliefs, while valuable social studies concepts and generalizations are examined.

Numerous opportunities for pointing out the important reality that diversity is normal and positive also exist. Open-ended discussions, for example, can help students determine life direction and can lead to increased self-understanding regarding their role as active and responsible citizens. Awareness of one's role as a global citizen may also be enhanced through such discussions.

Dealing with the affective aspects of education is a crucial responsibility of middle-level social studies educators and should form an important component of social studies programs.

Controversial Issues

There is little time and effort spent on controversial issues in social studies classes. Too little concern for addressing controversial issues is evident. Since "teachers' views tend to agree with the community view . . . teachers give up none of their integrity by not venturing too far into uncomfortable topics" (Shaver et al., 1979, p. 152). This problem seems to be one of growing seriousness, as our nation continues to drift toward more reactionary views and as political constraints hamper legitimate efforts to educate rather than simply train the school-age population.

We do not recommend a radical approach to middle grades social studies, but we do believe strongly that instruction in social studies must involve more than textbook reading and recitation. Active and responsible citizenship does not commence with graduation from high school or college. Early adolescents are citizens now and need to learn behaviors and develop attitudes and values that promote a deeper appreciation of the role of the citizen in a democratic environment.

Middle grades social studies teachers should make their classrooms a forum for democratic action and should not hesitate to address controversial issues that hold meaning for early adolescents (VanSickle, 1983). Community and social action projects and service-learning projects should be ongoing components of the social studies program.

Student Apathy

Teachers are genuinely concerned with the apathy so prevalent among students today. The national studies mentioned earlier confirm that social studies educators are indeed interested in the personal and academic well-being of their students. Why then do students appear apathetic toward social studies? One of the reasons is that teachers have not sufficiently drawn the connection between how early adolescents learn effectively and the instructional practices extant in their classrooms.

The unique needs and interests of this age group must be carefully considered when planning social studies programs and learning activities. As any successful middle grades educator can attest, apathy will quickly decrease when programming becomes more action-oriented.

A wide variety of teaching strategies should be utilized at the middle level, and materials should be selected in light of the multiplicity of needs and interests of early adolescents.

Skill Development

Too little emphasis is given to skill development in social studies classes. As noted previously, research suggests that textbooks are rarely challenged as an exercise in analysis. In addition, "tests typically emphasize textbook knowledge, rather than skill objectives" (Shaver et al., 1979, p. 151).

Often, class time is considered too valuable to be devoted to more time-consuming activities that contribute to building skills that are important for active and responsible citizenship (e.g., decision making; problem solving; critical thinking; locating, gathering, and evaluating information and ideas; and presenting ideas orally and in written form). These and other skills should be emphasized throughout the middle grades social studies curriculum, even at the expense of "covering" a predetermined course content.

Greater emphasis must be given to skill development in middle grades social studies. This emphasis should be a systematic and continuing aspect of all social studies curriculum and instruction.

Early Adolescent Development

Most middle-level teachers have insufficient knowledge of and professional preparation in the developmental period of early adolescence. This is a major reason that so many social studies classes closely resemble those of the senior high school.

The lack of knowledge about early adolescence certainly is not unique to social studies educators. The vast majority of current middle-level social studies teachers were prepared either as elementary or high school teachers, with little or no mention of the intermediate level (Alexander & McEwin, 1982, 1989).

Because of the still prevailing lack of middle-level teacher education programs, it is rare to find social studies educators who have received adequate preparation in early adolescence and know the related educational needs of their students. Studies of middle and junior high schools in several states revealed that only between 11% and 30% of teachers, respectively, had received special training for teaching at the middle level (Alexander & McEwin, 1989; Allen, 1980, 1981; Allen & Sheppard, 1990; McEwin, 1981).

As the majority of teachers, administrators, supervisors, and other personnel involved with middle-level social studies have little or no special preparation, extensive efforts should be made to provide information about early adolescents to them. Administrators and supervisors ought to assume responsibility for locating and making information available regarding early adolescents and how to best teach them.

Middle-level social studies teachers should be apprised of the developmental period of early adolescence by reading, attending conferences, and participating in other professional experiences that will increase their understanding of the students with whom they work. Administrators, supervisors, guidance personnel, and others responsible for instruction should make every effort to increase their own knowledge and assist other teachers in learning more about teaching early adolescents.

Student Personal Development

Social studies programs often do not contribute significantly to students' personal development. Although social studies properly emphasizes citizenship as it relates to government affairs, history, other social sciences, and the humanities, "much of the rhetoric of social-studies-as-citizenship, focusing on the goal of intelligent moral action in public affairs, negates a large part of the personal goals to which social studies more broadly construed could contribute" (Morrissett, 1981, p. 53).

By more closely relating social studies programs to the needs and interests of early adolescents, both the goals of personal development and specialized social studies knowledge can be attained more effectively. Every effort should be made to respect the uniqueness of each learner throughout the instructional process. Examples include: incorporating personal life experiences into social studies curricula; using students who have witnessed or participated in special events or who are of different ethnic backgrounds as unique resources; and providing opportunities to compare and contrast students' own developing attitude and value systems with those of other cultures.

Other examples for promoting both personal development and social studies include: keeping time journals; comparing one's self with historical figures; creating student exchange programs—even if limited to an immediate geographic location; providing a wealth of multicultural experiences; studying cultural variations throughout history; and providing ample opportunities for addressing students' newfound idealism by studying variability in human history. Finally, using children's literature is another way to promote increased understanding of active and responsible citizenship.

Middle grades social studies educators must recognize their responsibility to contribute to the personal development of students.

Becoming an Active Professional

Middle school social studies teachers need to become considerably more involved in professional associations. Administrators, supervisors, and other school-based personnel in support positions should also be involved and also actively encourage and financially support such involvement.

This would create an enlarged group with awareness of research results, teaching strategies, resource materials, and other aspects of professional functioning so important to quality instruction at the middle grades level. More extensive involvement will also make the professional associations they join more effective change agents in education. They need the input of classroom teachers to accomplish their goals. Association activities, publications, conferences, and other services offer opportunities for greater communication among middle grades social studies educators.

The Middle School Movement

The emergence of the middle school movement is having a positive effect on social studies instruction ("Social Studies in the Middle School," 1991; "Ability Grouping in Social Studies," 1992).

The reorganization of middle grades education in recent years has prompted increased attention on social studies education. Although a national study revealed that only limited significant instructional changes have occurred in most middle grades schools, advocates of the middle school concept have encouraged instructional and organizational changes that have had a positive impact on curriculum and instructional practices (Brooks & Edwards, 1978).

In schools utilizing the middle school concept, more emphasis is placed on interdisciplinary teaching and integrated units, personal development, cooperative and team teaching, and other components that simplify the planning and implementation of meaningful social studies programs (Merenbloom, 1991). It remains to be seen whether the middle school movement will have a lasting impact on social studies.

Aspects of the middle school concept should be examined by social studies educators, regardless of their current school organization plan, to determine if these concepts may be beneficial to their teaching. Cooperative planning and teaching, flexible scheduling, and heterogeneous grouping hold great potential for improving the effectiveness of social studies programs and for promoting active and responsible citizenship among early adolescents ("Ability Grouping in Social Studies," 1992).

Final Thoughts

This chapter explores several of the issues facing middle grades social studies. We challenge you to further reflect on key issues and to search for improved ways to provide meaningful social studies experiences for early adolescents.

All of us face a profound responsibility for preparing young people for living not only now, but also well into the twenty-first century. Social studies educators especially are charged with the task of preparing youth for active and responsible citizenship. No more important task exists. Planting a legacy of reflection coupled with the abilities and desires to nourish personal powers is a powerful goal indeed.

Reflecting on our discussion in Chapter 2 regarding the value of history, we are reminded how important it is to consider the historical and philosophical record that guides current perspectives and realities on schooling. Such understanding may remind us not only of the ends we seek through the educational enterprise, but also that all too often we may have developed policies and practices that run counter to our stated goals (Hullfish & Smith, 1961).

THE MIDDLE SCHOOL CONNECTION: QUESTIONS TO PONDER

For Preservice Students

1. Do you agree with Alexander's broad goals for middle grades education? Explain your response(s).
2. Reflect on what goals seemed to be operating in the school environment when you were in the middle grades. What were some of these goals?
3. Should early adolescents be empowered in the manner Toepfer describes? If so, how might such empowerment be realized? If not, why?
4. Was such empowerment a part of your middle grades experience? Explain your response.
5. In a small-group setting, discuss your reactions to each of the current realities in social studies education. Which of these realities were reflected in your personal middle grades social studies experience?
6. Do any of the findings about the state of social studies education surprise you? If yes, which ones and why?
7. Reflect on each of the conclusions and related recommendations offered in this chapter. Share your reactions to each with your peers.
8. Do any of the conclusions and recommendations challenge you to rethink your perspective on what constitutes good middle grades social studies curriculum and instruction? If so, how?
9. To what degree does your vision of good teaching and learning reflect any of the perspectives presented in Chapter 1.

For Inservice Students

1. Do you agree with Alexander's broad goals for middle grades education? Explain your response(s).
2. How do the goals of your middle grades school compare to Alexander's? Discuss both the similarities and differences.
3. How are the goals that guide the organization of your middle grades school operationalized on a day-to-day basis?
4. Should your early adolescent students be empowered in the manner Toepfer describes? Explain your response.
5. Does your middle grades school promote such empowerment? If so, how? If not, why?
6. Discuss your reactions to the current realities in social studies education as described in this chapter.
7. To what extent are the current realities reflected in your school's social studies curriculum and instructional practices? Explain your response.
8. Do any of the findings concerning current realities surprise you? If yes, which one(s) and why?
9. Share with colleagues your reflections on each of the conclusions and recommendations in this chapter.
10. To what extent do any of the conclusions and recommendations challenge you to change your school's social studies program?
11. To what degree do any of the conclusions and recommendations challenge you to change your instructional behavior?
12. How does your teaching behavior reflect any of the perspectives offered in Chapter 1?
13. To what degree does your school's climate reflect any of the perspectives offered in Chapter 1?

FOOD FOR THOUGHT BEFORE MOVING ON

Discuss your responses to these questions with colleagues and others interested in improving middle grades social studies in your school. Ask your students how they feel about social studies in general, as well as what type of social studies experiences they believe will promote a more active and responsible citizenship.

1. When was the last time you seriously reflected on the state of social studies education in your school? In your district? In your state?
2. When was the last time you analyzed the degree of consistency between your teaching and the series of recommendations offered in this chapter? Explain your response.

REFERENCES

"Ability Grouping in Social Studies." (1992). NCSS Position Statement. *Social Education, 56*(5):268–270.

Alexander, William. (1988). "School in the Middle: Rhetoric and Reality." *Social Education, 53*(2):107–109.

Alexander, William, and Paul George. (1981). *The Exemplary Middle School.* New York: Holt, Rinehart and Winston.

Alexander, William, and C. Kenneth McEwin. (1982). "Toward Middle Level Teacher Education." *Middle School Journal, 13*:3–5.

Alexander, William, and C. Kenneth McEwin. (1989). *Schools in the Middle: Status and Progress.* Columbus, OH: National Middle School Association.

Allen, Michael. (1980). *Vermont–New Hampshire Middle Grades Survey: A Report.* ERIC. ED 198 089.

Allen, Michael. (1981). *Maine Middle Grades Survey: A Report.* Boone, NC: Appalachian State University.

Allen, Michael. (1989). "Reflections on the Vermont Design: Implications for Middle Level Education." *NELMS Journal, 2*(1):42–43.

Allen, Michael, and Ronnie Sheppard. (1990). *Profile of Georgia Schools in the Middle: A Research Report.* Georgia Middle School Association and Georgia Association of Middle School Principals.

Beane, James. (1994). *A Middle School Curriculum: From Rhetoric to Reality,* 2nd ed. Columbus, OH: National Middle School Association.

Brooks, Kenneth, and F. Edwards. (1978). *The Middle School in Transition: A Research Report on the Status of the Middle School Movement.* Lexington: The Center for Professional Development, University of Kentucky.

Carnegie Council on Adolescent Development. (1989). *Turning Points: Preparing American Youth for the 21st Century.* New York: Carnegie Council on Adolescent Development, Carnegie Corporation of New York.

George, Paul, and William Alexander. (1993). *The Exemplary Middle School,* 2nd ed. New York: Holt, Rinehart and Winston.

Hullfish, H. Gordon, and Philip Smith. (1961). *Reflective Thinking: The Method of Education.* New York: Dodd, Mead.

Lewbel, Samuel. (1989). *Interdisciplinary Units in New England's Middle Schools: A How-To Guide.* Rowley, MA: New England League of Middle Schools.

Lounsbury, John, and J. Howard Johnston. (1988). *Life in the Three 6th Grades.* Reston, VA: National Association of Secondary School Principals.

McEwin, C. Kenneth. (1981). *A Report on Middle Grades Schools in North Carolina: A Study of Current Practices.* Monograph #2. Boone: The North Carolina League of Middle/Junior High Schools. ERIC. ED 199 206.

Merenbloom, Elliot. (1991). *The Team Process: A Handbook for Teachers,* 3rd ed. Columbus, OH: National Middle School Association.

Morrissett, Irvin. (1981). "The Needs of the Future and the Constraints of the Past." In Howard Mehlinger and O. L. Davis, eds., *The Social Studies,* Eighteenth Yearbook. Chicago: National Society of the Study of Education.

Shaver, James, O. L. Davis, and Susan Helburn. (1979). "The Status of Social Studies Education: Impressions from Three NSF Studies." *Social Education, 43*(2):150–153.

"Social Studies in the Middle School: A Report of the Task Force on Social Studies in the Middle School." (1991). *Social Education, 55*(5):287–293.

Stake, R., and J. Easley. (1978). *Case Studies in Science Education: Report to the National Science Foundation.* Center for Instructional Research and Curriculum Evaluation and Committee on Culture and Cognition, University of Illinois at Urbana-Champaign. Washington, DC: U.S. Government Printing Office. #036 000 00377 and 038 000 00376-3.

Stevens, Robert. (1990). *Gavels to Gravestones: Seven Middle School Social Studies Activities.* Rowley, MA: New England League of Middle Schools.

Stevenson, Chris. (1992). *Teaching the Ten to Fourteen Year Old.* White Plains, NY: Longman.

This We Believe. (1992). Columbus, OH: National Middle School Association.

Toepfer, Conrad. (1988). "What to Know about Young Adolescents." *Social Education, 53*(2):110–112.

VanSickle, Ronald. (1983). "Practicing What We Teach: Promoting Democratic Experiences in the Classroom." In Mary Hepburn, ed., *Democratic Education in Schools and Classrooms.* Washington, DC: National Council for the Social Studies.

Vars, Gordon. (1987). *Interdisciplinary Teaching in the Middle Grades: Why and How.* Columbus, OH: National Middle School Association.

Weiss, J. (1978). *Report of the 1977 National Survey of Science, Mathematics, and Social Studies Education.* National Science Foundation. Washington, DC: U.S. Government Printing Office. #038 000 00364-0.

Wiley, Kenneth. (1977). *The Status of Pre-College Science, Mathematics, and Social Studies Education: 1955–1975.* Report to the National Science Foundation, Social Science Education Consortium, #038 000 00363-1. Washington, DC: U.S. Government Printing Office.

2

THE NATURE OF SOCIAL STUDIES

Remember when you

- thought Los Angeles, Miami, London, and Boston were states?
- studied current events every Friday?
- constructed a military fort out of matchsticks, or a flour, salt, and water map of Latin America?
- memorized important facts such as state capitals, the Preamble of the United States Constitution, and products of various countries?
- read your social studies textbook from the beginning to end and answered questions at the end of each chapter?
- depended primarily on the *World Book* or *Encyclopedia Britannica* for oral or written reports on such topics as Indians, Eskimos, or the Civil War?
- could not pronounce, much less spell, the names of the capital cities of most African nations?

From its rather inauspicious beginning in the 1800s as the teaching of certain patriotic values through myth and moral parables, social studies has experienced a checkered history. As an important component of the public school curriculum since the early twentieth century, it has remained just a fragmented aspect of the total school curriculum. And so it continues today.

A cursory review of the professional literature reveals a field rife with conflict and disagreement. Social studies continues to be the target of efforts to indoctrinate or otherwise inculcate the youth of the nation with proper values, attitudes, and beliefs of a particular way of life, or promote a specific social, political, or environmental agenda.

Regardless of the particular view held by individuals, students generally are turned off by traditional approaches to teaching social studies. Social studies vies with English (reading and grammar) as the least liked subject by young adolescents. For both teachers and students, a necessary first step toward renewal is a reassessment of the goals and objectives of the middle grades social studies curriculum.

The social studies traditions best describe the various emphases and competing conceptions of the field. An important outcome of analyzing these traditions is a workable definition of social studies and a better understanding of the current situation in the field.

THE FOUR SOCIAL STUDIES TRADITIONS

A significant publication, *Defining the Social Studies* (Barr, Barth, & Shermis, 1977), outlines the various philosophical theories that have woven themselves through social studies since its inception. The authors delineate a "four traditions" approach to the field in an effort to understand the competing philosophical perspectives in social studies. Using this model, they trace the historical and philosophical antecedents of social studies in the United States. The four traditions identified are: (1) social studies taught as citizenship transmission, (2) social studies taught as social science, (3) social studies taught as reflective inquiry, and (4) social studies taught as personal development (Miller & Young, 1979). A brief description of the characteristics of each tradition follows.

Social Studies Taught as Citizenship Transmission

This tradition is the oldest and most pervasive of the four traditions. Research suggests that the majority of social studies curriculum and instructional practices in schools reflect it. It also enjoys wide public support.

The *purpose* of this tradition is that a particular conception of social studies be both learned and believed (Barr, Barth, & Shermis, 1977). Essentially, "truth and knowledge" reside with the teacher and with a particular textbook selected to be studied and to be integrated into the student's growing understanding of the world.

The *method* employed by teachers consists of a series of techniques and strategies that involve a mixture of description and persuasion. According to the authors, this tradition is "dedicated to transmitting a precisely defined image of society and of citizenship" (Barr et al., 1977, p. 60).

The *content* of the tradition is based on knowledge, assumptions, and beliefs that are accepted, generally, by the larger society. In essence, this means that whatever is found in the textbook and subsequently interpreted by the teacher and students is accepted as a reasonable explanation of reality.

Social Studies Taught as Social Science

The second tradition rose to prominence during the new social studies era of the 1960s. Although a number of school districts and states redesigned their social studies programs and curriculum guidelines around the social science model, the tradition did not have the far-reaching impact its developers and supporters envisioned.

The *purpose* of the tradition is "that young people shall acquire the knowledge, skills, and devices of particular social science disciplines to the end that they become effective citizens" (Barr et al., 1977, pp. 61–62). The implicit assumption is that good citizenship results from learning the structure and methods of the various social science disciplines—two highly questionable assumptions.

The *method* employed is a distillation, for teaching purposes, of the various models of inquiry used by social scientists in their quest for knowledge.

The *content* of the tradition consists of specific topics, issues, and problems of the various social sciences that have been conceptualized for specific grade levels.

Social Studies Taught as Reflective Inquiry

The third tradition, though not new, is a significant departure from the first two. Beyond the fact that the stated purpose is the same as the first two traditions, all similarity ends. The *purpose*—the duties of citizenship—is defined as the ability to make good decisions within a given sociopolitical context.

Proponents of reflective inquiry make little distinction between method and content. Essentially, the *method* is a type of inquiry that promotes decision making, problem solving and enhances questioning in a divergent context for the purpose of arriving at satisfactory answers to important problems. The problems and issues selected form the *content* studied in this tradition.

Social Studies Taught as Personal Development

Another view of social studies (Miller & Young, 1979) offers a different philosophical orientation to the field. The *purpose* of this tradition is self-development and human interaction, rather than the accumulation of information and traditional values. Simply stated, the goal is to help students discover in themselves the universal experiences of the human race.

Through a *method* of inquiry called introspection, the tradition seeks to assist students in discovering their own essences and becoming autonomous, self-directed learners cognizant of their past and future. Introspection includes observing and analyzing one's own mental states and processes, one's own thoughts and feelings, as well as a personal conception of truths derived from sense perception, logical demonstration, scientific proof, intuition, or revelation, which all occur in the particular sociopolitical context of the individual.

The *content* of the tradition is designed to enrich the understanding of the learner's inner self, rather than to produce a conformist, activist, or social scientist. The content is based on the social sciences and humanities. Such an approach includes a curriculum strong in decision-making opportunities coupled with high expectations of individual, intellectual, and social responsibility.

The teacher's responsibility and involvement is to assist learners in maximizing both their intellectual and social-emotional potential.

Although some aspects of each tradition may be found in most middle schools and high schools, one will probably predominate. Which tradition seems to reflect your curricular and instructional attitudes or practices?

SOCIAL STUDIES: A DEFINITION

Social studies has been described as simplified social science, a fusion and integration of the social sciences, instruction in patriotism, and value inculcation, to name but a few. Until recently, there has been no serious discussion of or widespread agreement on a definition of social studies. Disagreement in the field has extended beyond a theoretical argument over goals, objectives, and appropriate content into the classroom, where teachers are faced with a bewildering array of options and expectations for fulfilling the task of educating students for active and responsible citizenship in a democratic environment (*Charting a Course: Social Studies for the 21st Century*, 1989).

This problem is particularly acute at the middle level, because it is here that most students are introduced to their first serious and systematic interaction with social studies as a formal course. It behooves middle grades teachers to address the curricular and instructional issues in social studies seriously.

In spite of a plethora of definitions, it is the one offered in *Defining the Social Studies* (Barr et al., 1977) that we believe holds the most promise of enhancing social studies at the middle level:

> The social studies is an integration of experience and knowledge concerning human relations for the purpose of citizenship education.
>> The goal: Citizenship Education
>> Objectives required to achieve effective citizenship:
>
> 1. Knowledge
> 2. Skills necessary to process information

3. Values and beliefs
4. Social participation. (Barr et al., 1977, p. 69)

From this framework for organizing and defining the social studies, one may derive a distinctive view of the field as it relates to middle grades curriculum and instruction. We discuss the definition in relation to appropriate learning experiences for middle-level students.

KNOWLEDGE

Although the knowledge gained through a study of social studies varies, depending on one's philosophical view, there is a thread of commonality regarding the importance of the social sciences to the social studies. The social science disciplines form a major portion of the knowledge base of social studies.

Traditionally, the focus has been on history and geography, as reflected in the content of the textbooks used in most classrooms. The 1960s witnessed a veritable tidal wave of involvement by social scientists in the development of social studies curricula. The force propelling this involvement was the desire to infuse social studies with more academic rigor. This movement is characterized by the second tradition, *social studies taught as social science.*

Focusing on the social sciences alone, however, is insufficient if middle grades social studies is to take on a new and vibrant meaning and value for students. The knowledge base must be expanded to include the humanities, as well as the personal life experiences of early adolescents.

The Social Sciences

Social sciences may be defined by two main aspects: the *structure of each discipline* (hard data, principles, and assumptions) and the *modes of inquiry* or processes employed in gaining new knowledge. Educationally speaking, social science concepts and generalizations and the methods used to generate them are important to social studies.

History

As Heilbroner wrote, "when we estrange ourselves from history, we do not enlarge, we diminish ourselves, even as individuals. We subtract from our lives one meaning which they do in fact possess, whether we recognize it or not. We cannot help living in history. We can only fail to be aware of it" (Heilbroner, 1960, p. 209).

History is both a record of humankind's past and the past itself. In a very real sense, history enjoys an existence apart from our knowledge of it. It is important that teachers and students realize that recorded history has come to us filtered through the minds of observers and writers and, therefore, is often one-sided and biased. There is much truth in the statement that history has been written by the victor, not the vanquished. Clearly, history is a subject with a strong interpretive component.

In spite of these necessary caveats, the "organization of history has a kind of elementary simplicity about it that has been long irresistible to teachers and textbook writers. This most often results in a chronological approach to the teaching of history that focuses on historical fact" (Commager & Muessig, 1980, p. 14). Such teaching seldom moves beyond memorization of discrete, often unrelated facts.

An additional important consideration is the development of an appreciation for the "many and sobering limitations on historical material" (Commager & Muessig, 1980, p. 43), particularly since these limitations extend to textbooks used in social studies classrooms. History is often terribly distorted, because it is the product of the human mind and is principally a written record subject to all the vagaries of that form of information transmission.

In fact, the patterns of history are not an inherent part of the unfolding of history, but artificial designations imposed by the observer and writer as they make their best effort to bring clarity and meaning to an otherwise jumbled mass of human experience. Such patterns too often become ends in themselves in the sense that the reader comes to believe that "this is the way it really happened" or "these are the actual causes of this or that event."

Finally, the temptation to view historical events from a "present-mindedness" is a limiting factor for teachers and students alike. It is easy to play "Monday morning quarterback" when reading about the past. We should remain cognizant of the tendency to judge events and people's motivations from our own personal perspectives.

Once teachers admit to themselves "that history is neither scientific nor mechanical, that the historian is human and therefore fallible, and that the ideal history, completely objective and dispassionate, is an illusion" (Commager & Muessig, 1980, p. 49), they are free to explore the varieties of history in ways that will breathe life into their teaching and enable them to adequately answer the age-old question, "Why do we have to study this?"

Through the study of history, early adolescents' natural curiosity and spirit of inquiry can be excited and lead them to growth beyond the immediate and to achieve a deeper appreciation of the past (*Building a History Curriculum*, 1988). Studying history is important to the development of "attitudes of mind that distinguish the educated man—the habits of skepticism and criticism; of thinking with perspective and objectivity; of judging the good and the bad and the in-between in human affairs; of weighing the pros and cons and discerning the different shades of gray that lie between gray and black" (Daniels, 1972, pp. 8–9).

What meaning, then, do such remarks hold for middle grades learners and teachers? They suggest that we need to move away from indoctrination, the glorification of the nation-state, and attempts to condition students to "automatic loyalties." Furthermore, it points to the importance of promoting an enlightened understanding and appreciation of individual freedom and responsibility and the realities of living in a global context.

Such an attitude would enhance life and help students become more active and responsible citizens. It also denotes the importance of promoting, through instructional processes and teacher behavior, tolerance for differences in loyalties, cultures, faiths, and human ideals.

From Theory to Practice: Some Possibilities. In studying history, early adolescents ought to have opportunities to examine the whys and wherefores of the discipline. This may be accomplished through an independent reading of both primary and secondary historical documents and related sources, independent study and research on various topics and writings from various perspectives such as autobiography and biography, and reporting on historical events of particular interest. Use of documents from the National Archives is an excellent way to teach important historical facts and the fine art of historical interpretation (*Teaching with Documents*, 1989).

Students can be encouraged to become historical Sherlock Holmeses. The process of collecting, interpreting, and explaining historical evidence is an excellent way to promote inductive reasoning. Teachers can initiate this whole process by such techniques as local history projects, various reading materials, field trips, and simulation games. Furthermore, the historical record is replete with famous quotations that prove intriguing to students and often lead to further study and deliberation.

Geography

In recent years, geography, particularly regional or place geography, has enjoyed a modest revival in schools (*Guidelines for Geographic Education*, 1984; National Geography Standards, 1994; *Curriculum Update: Geography's Renaissance*, Spring 1996). This trend is positive, considering that we are a geographically illiterate nation. Although television brings into focus the world and its problems on a daily basis, many fail to appreciate the fact that ours is a global age. The danger exists that in efforts to become less ethnocentric there may be a tendency to return to teaching geography the "old way."

Geography has too often consisted of the study of landforms, climate, and various agricultural, mineral, and industrial products of individual nations. Unfortunately, the majority of textbooks reflect such emphases. Although it is of some value to develop this kind of mental picture of individual nations and peoples, it is far more important to grasp the essence of the global nature of our existence, the interdependence of life on the planet, and the impact of different lifestyles on the lives of others (Manson & Ridd, 1977).

Essentially, geography and other social sciences share an interest in people. Geography can be exciting when people, their culture, and their response to the environments in which they exist are understood in a global sense. Understanding the interrelations between places makes geography come alive.

Gone are the days of political and economic hegemony when people could maintain a high degree of ethnocentrism. The overriding reality today is interdependence—essential reliance on one another in all areas of life. An issue related to the need to understand interdependence is found in the process of environmental destruction throughout the world. Through the study of various environmental issues as they relate to geography, students are better able to grasp the interrelatedness of life on earth.

In addition to emphasizing people, places, and the global nature of life and interdependence, geography emphasizes certain skills essential to a sound social studies education, such as map reading and interpretation and the understanding of time and distance. Unfortunately, "evidence increasingly indicates that many students are not learning much about either geography or map interpretation" (Chapin & Gross, 1963, p. 107).

What do such developments mean for middle-level social studies teachers? First, the study of countries around the world as though they were separate, independent geographic entities should be deemphasized. The concept of interdependence should be stressed, along with skill work in map and globe reading and interpretation. Such an approach to geography focuses on a more comprehensive view of humankind and its surroundings.

From Theory to Practice: Some Possibilities.   In helping students develop a deeper appreciation of geographic information and concepts, teachers should "focus on the interaction of cultural forms and natural environment" (Joyce, 1972, p. 123). In learning about climates, vegetation, natural resources, and landforms, students should be helped to see how different cultures have adapted to their physical environment.

In addition to learning about the relationship between people and their environments, students should learn to appreciate and use generalizations important to geography. For example,

1. People live on the Earth, which is located in a solar system in the universe.
2. Each area of the earth possesses unique geographic characteristics.
3. All people have in common the need for food, clothing, and shelter.
4. In the struggle to survive, people are forced to interact directly with their physical environment.

5. The physical environment, although affected by people, also has a limiting effect on them.
6. Cultural groups meet their needs in unique ways that depend on available resources and their own value systems.
7. The concept of interdependence may be understood particularly by the uneven distribution of the wide variety of natural resources people employ to meet their needs.
8. Cultural patterns change over time as the result of changing geographic patterns.
9. The earth has been radically altered by cultural patterns.

Students must be made aware of both the global nature and interdependence of existence on this planet and the infinite number of direct relationships between their communities and those around the globe. Excellent examples of lessons and activities in geography may be found in Chapters 5 and 6.

Anthropology

Anthropology, the study of people and their works, plays a minor role in most middle grades social studies curriculum but should be an important part of the academic experience at this level. As a discipline devoted to the study of group life, it is divided into several subdisciplines. A brief description of each follows.

Physical anthropology is the study of the physical aspects of humankind as a living entity, with particular emphasis on the evidence about the evolution of humankind. Archaeology is concerned with the careful analysis of data on human cultures gained through "excavation of sites of former human habitations—ancient dwellings, monuments, objects of art, tools, weapons, and other human works covered over by the soil of time" (Pelto & Muessig, 1980, p. 2).

Anthropologists are also interested in *linguistics*—the study of language—as language, in its multitude of forms, has served as the primary mode of communication among people. *Cultural anthropology* is concerned with the many varieties of human behavior, past and present, that are found throughout the world.

Because of its emphasis on people in group settings, anthropology has much in common with sociology. Nevertheless, these two disciplines do differ in several important ways. The anthropologist generally is interested in the study of non-Western peoples, whereas sociologists tend to study aspects of Western culture. Anthropologists prefer to conduct research on group life in face-to-face contact (ethnographic studies), whereas sociologists generally study larger segments of a particular social system.

Probably the most important aspects of anthropology for middle grades teachers and students are: (1) the concept of culture, and (2) the nature and methods of fieldwork of the dig. Although anthropology is a young discipline and cannot claim to have produced extensive and elaborate laws or generalizations about human behavior, several postulates have been developed. They include the following:

1. Culture is a total way of life, not just a superficial set of customs. It largely shapes how we feel, behave, and perceive as we adapt to our world.
2. Every cultural system is an interconnected series of ideas and patterns for behavior in which changes in one aspect generally lead to changes in other segments of the system.
3. Every human cultural system is logical and coherent in its own terms, given the basic assumptions and knowledge available to the given community.
4. Study of almost any behaviors and beliefs among nonmodern peoples, no matter how unusual, is of direct relevance to understanding our own culture, for it appears that humans everywhere shape their beliefs and behaviors in response to the same fundamental human problems.
5. Many traditional cultural practices and beliefs that once seemed quaint and outmoded have been found to have a pragmatic basis.
6. Individuals, even in small-scale traditional societies, differ one from another in attitudes, information, skills, culturally valued resources, and other attributes.
7. Although the peoples of the world may be roughly (and arbitrarily) categorized into major population groups, based on a very limited number of physical characteristics, there are no "pure races" and there never have been.
8. There is no evidence of significant differences in ability or "intelligence" among the major ethnic or "racial" groupings of the world (Pelto & Muessig, 1980).

With these postulates, students may begin to develop a deeper understanding of culture and its ramifications. In addition, such understanding should extend to non-Western cultures. Anthropology shares with geography the task of helping us become less ethnocentric in our life views.

From Theory to Practice: Some Possibilities.   One of the most exciting aspects of anthropology lies in the fieldwork of archaeologists. Duplicating the conditions and techniques of an archaeological excavation around the school ground is not difficult. A series of artifacts can be buried, and students can enjoy a dig. Through this experience, students learn the necessity of taking great care of excavated materials, while paying close attention to the position and context of each object.

From the dig comes the opportunity to analyze materials and objects in a given context, while learning how to read and describe the story of the excavated materials. Field trips to dump sites around old farmhouses are an excellent way to introduce students to the study of human activity from an anthropological perspective. Such experiences also help students to develop an appreciation for the difficulties of life in the past.

Another excellent way to motivate students to study and understand other cultures is through the literature and art of different cultures.

Sociology

Sociology is the social science discipline most closely related to the developmental realities of early adolescence in the sense that many of the processes studied by sociologists are directly experienced by early adolescents. Sociology is the study of human behavior in a group setting, with an emphasis on the study of groups in the Western world. Like the other social sciences, sociology concerns itself with people.

Sociologists study the organization of society from the perspective of the social structures within each society. The basic elements of a social structure are norms, roles, and positions—all of which are important facets of the proper functioning of any group or society. The study of social structure is relevant to early adolescents in their endeavor to gain a more comprehensive understanding of society and their role in it. Sociologists are also concerned with human interaction, the principal component of social life.

Learning that one can predict the behavior of other people and that this predictability enables people to function in the group setting is important for middle grades students. Finally, sociologists are interested in the process of socialization, "the procedures by which the individual is taught the skills, attitudes, and values necessary for proper participation in his or her society" (Kitchens & Muessig, 1980, p. 15). The principal agents of socialization—the family, school, peer group, mass media, and church—are important in the work of sociologists and, therefore, should constitute a significant part of the middle grades social studies curriculum.

As is true with history, students often ask about the value of studying sociological concepts. There are at least three good reasons for studying sociology. First, sociology can "enable individuals to understand the historical forces that help create events in their life" (Kitchens & Muessig, 1980, p. 57). Such understanding helps promote self-understanding. Second, the study of sociological concepts, norms, roles, and positions promotes a deeper understanding of other people. This is important for middle grades students, given the developmental realities they face. Third, "the study of sociology (teaches) the definition of a host of commonly used words . . . (such as) alienation, institution, interaction, social change, crowds, rumors, community and urban" (Kitchens & Muessig, 1980, p. 59).

From Theory to Practice: Some Possibilities.   Two important considerations for middle grades social studies teachers in their efforts to promote deeper understanding and appreciation for sociology are to help students investigate and understand the socialization process and to grasp, in a practical sense, the concept of norms. The use of literature—fiction and nonfiction alike—is an excellent vehicle for such learning.

Economics

In recent years, the study of economics has found its way into the social studies curriculum. Characterized by many as the most difficult of the social sciences to understand, economics often frightens even the most courageous social studies educator. This misunderstanding and fear of economics has been ameliorated somewhat by the excellent work of the Joint Council for Economic Education.

Briefly, economics may be defined as "a study of the choice-making process used by individuals and total societies in their attempt to satisfy their needs and wants for goods and services" (Warmke & Muessig, 1980, p. 1). More simply stated, economics is the study of how people earn and spend money.

The basic economic questions faced by people and nations are "WHAT goods and services should be produced; HOW should these goods and services be produced; HOW MUCH should be produced; and, FOR WHOM should the goods and services be produced?" (Warmke & Muessig, 1980, p. 4).

Economics, then, involves the analysis of these *what, how, how much,* and *for whom* questions. Developing an understanding of the many ways in which societies have answered these questions provides one with a degree of economics literacy. As with the other social sciences, economics concerns itself with people. Specifically, it is concerned with how people answer the four previous questions.

From Theory to Practice: Some Possibilities.   Middle grades students need to study the basic concepts and generalization of economics in order to better understand how personal, local, state, national, and international economies function. Only then will they begin to grasp the relationship between their lives and the discipline. With such knowledge comes the opportunity to be more active, responsible citizens and more intelligent consumers.

Integrating the following generalizations into the ongoing curriculum helps students develop a working knowledge of economics:

1. Goods and services are essential for survival.
2. Scarcity—the result of the gap between wants and needs and limited resources—causes conflicts.

3. Every society must decide what goods and services to produce. The answer varies from society to society.
4. Each society must determine how goods and services are to be produced. This also varies from society to society.
5. Every society must determine how much to produce.
6. Every society must determine who gets what goods and services.
7. Economic specialization throughout the world has promoted increased trade and interdependence among countries.
8. The medium of exchange varies from society to society. For most it is some form of money (Warmke & Muessig, 1980).

For teachers faced with teaching economic literacy, an important consideration is to foster economic awareness through newspapers, vocabulary work, reading assignments, and class discussions. A variety of simulation games are designed to teach students about concepts of scarcity and about allocations and choices necessitated by scarcity.

An important consideration in economics that is shared with the other social sciences is the reality of interdependence. An in-depth analysis of communities around the world is a way to teach students about the complex web of interdependence. The questions asked by economists also contain a significant value component.

Political Science

Political science endeavors to "develop a systematic knowledge about some aspect of the world with a focus on government" (Straayer, 1980, p. 1).

Political scientists begin their study with the following proposition:

> that people value and desire different things; that human wants are insatiable, while goods and values are limited; and, as a result, conflict is inevitable. Among the human inventions that deal with conflicts are governments. The processes by which people seek to influence governments and by which governmental institutions make and administer decisions, they term politics. (Straayer, 1980, p. 2)

Other areas of interest for the political scientist include the various roles citizens play in the governing process, the contents of public policy, and the relationships between governments.

Frequently, the question is asked, "What good is the study of political science?" Although various responses are possible, the following response seems most appropriate. Straayer (1980) suggests that the teaching of government and politics helps to create the informed citizenry necessary for the maintenance of a democratic policy and contributes to the development and maintenance of a more humane and civil society, and that the knowledge generated by students of government and politics improves collective choices by helping decision makers avoid what might otherwise be the unanticipated and unwanted consequences of their actions.

From Theory to Practice: Some Possibilities.   An important consideration in social studies instruction is the desirability of producing learners who:

1. have developed a global view in their attitudes and values
2. demonstrate a commitment to democratic processes and behavior
3. are reflective in the development and implementation of their political views
4. are informed and committed to active political involvement
5. are personally and socially responsible (Straayer, 1980)

The process of integrating these characteristics into the daily behavior and belief systems of students may be enhanced through studying interest groups, bureaucracies and bureaucratic processes, and newspaper political cartoons.

More important, efforts to develop democratic attitudes and commitment to rational processes for solving problems are aided immeasurably when students are exposed to school environments in which freedom, openness, and responsible behavior prevail (Hepburn, 1983).

The Humanities

Without question, the humanities offer rich material for enhancing middle-level social studies education. The humanities, including literature, languages, painting, sculpture, music, dance, and theater, are vital to the study of the myriad of culture groups throughout the world. Furthermore, the humanities lend themselves to team teaching, given their interdisciplinary nature. Opportunities to integrate humanities into the extant social studies curriculum also abound (Smith, Monson, & Dobson, 1992).

The judicious use of literature is an excellent way to promote a deeper appreciation of global realities, interdependence, and the overriding similarities among the people of the world. Studying a nation's art, language, music, and other aspects of culture are exciting and important components of sound social studies programming (Art and Humanities in the Social Studies, 1995).

From Theory to Practice: Some Possibilities.   An excellent way to initiate a social studies unit is to listen to the music of the culture being studied. Pictures of artwork, sculpture, and architecture will inject life into how students represent that culture. Children's literature from around the world is another excellent way to introduce people to other cultures.

Personal Life Experiences

Another important source of knowledge in social studies is the personal life experiences that early adolescents bring to the instructional setting. In our age of travel and mass media, few students remain completely ignorant of the world beyond their immediate community.

Rare is the group of students that does not include at least some individuals who have traveled out-of-state or out-of-nation. Many have relatives in other states or nations and have traveled to other geographic areas, returning with an expanded perspective and a deeper appreciation for the similarities among people. Tapping students' life experiences opens a world of instructional possibilities.

The day-by-day reality of meeting basic needs and living in a family setting, a community, and society are common to most people. Such realities are rich fodder for expanding knowledge. Involving students in social studies in meaningful ways by providing opportunities to integrate their life experiences into the curriculum adds vitality to learning and provides more reason to learn.

SKILLS NECESSARY TO PROCESS INFORMATION

Decision making should be a major and active consideration in the middle grades social studies curriculum. In addition to learning the steps to decision making, students need to practice the skill daily.

Decision making is usually understood as the process of making "reasoned choices from among several alternatives" (Cassidy & Kurfman, 1977, p. 1). This definition presupposes sufficient, available, and sound information, as well as opportunities to consider all reasonable alternatives.

In spite of statements to the contrary, most research supports the contention that decision making is not an explicit part of the ongoing social studies experiences for middle grades students (Lounsbury & Johnston, 1988). In addition to the need for informed citizens, "the extent to which we provide . . . (middle grades) students with decision-making skills" helps them to "fulfill their individual potential and build self-esteem on which healthy personalities are based" (Cassiday & Kurfman, 1977, p. 4).

Through the systematic development of skills necessary to process information, students should also develop various abilities:

1. (through) an information base in history and the social sciences . . . make connections among previously learned and new information.
2. think using different logical patterns and perspectives obtained through the study of history and the social sciences.

3. recognize that new knowledge is created by their interaction with new information from history or the social sciences.
4. learn to communicate with others about the data and interpretations of history and the social sciences as applied to their studies and to the real world. (Bragaw & Hartoonian, 1988, pp. 12–14)[1]

Another aspect of decision making is found in the reality of early adolescent development. This is a time of challenging personal decisions. Decisions concerning their future, physical and social development, responses to peer pressure, and their place in the world are a persistent part of everyday life for early adolescents. Practice in making decisions in both the personal and academic setting is an essential ingredient to developing the ability to make sound, informed decisions.

Finally, interest in skill development in social studies has promoted a continuing stream of essential skills for the field. One of the most recent includes the following general categories:

1. skills related to acquiring information including reading, study, reference and information search, and technical skills unique to electronic devices;
2. skills related to organizing and using information including thinking, decision making, and metacognitive skills; and,
3. skills related to interpersonal relationships, including personal, group interaction, social and political participation skills. ("In Search of a Scope and Sequence," 1989, pp. 386–387)

VALUES AND BELIEFS

The issue of values has traditionally been a volatile one in our public schools. Officially, the position is one of value neutrality, particularly in social studies. Furthermore, there is an "official" effort to refrain from indoctrination. Although it is generally believed that public schools demand objectivity and guard carefully against any type of indoctrination, any social institution charged with the task of socialization can hardly refrain from some sort of overt or covert values inculcation or orientation.

The very nature of the educational enterprise demands involvement with values and value-related issues. The question is not whether values are going to be addressed, but how they are to be addressed. In the 1970s and 1980s, the field of values education experienced an explosion of methods and tech-

---

[1]For an expanded discussion of these and related points, see Bragaw and Hartoonian (1988).

niques for dealing with value-related issues in the classroom. Such growth has not been without problems.

Principally, the problems in the field relate to confusion over terms, the role of the school in teaching values, the lack of carefully trained people to use the newly developed materials, the singular lack of appropriate evaluation procedures for measuring the impact of the values-related materials, the massive volume of materials available, and maybe most important, which values the schools ought to represent or reflect in daily activity.

Among the multitude of approaches to values—evocation, inculcation, awareness, moral reasoning, analysis, clarification, commitment, and union (Superka, 1974)—the values-clarification approach has enjoyed widespread acceptance because it focuses more on the valuing process (Curwin & Curwin, 1974; Howe & Howe, 1975) than on promoting a specific set of values. Certainly, values clarification is not without its detractors. Some feel that values clarification is a form of subtle manipulation, whereby certain values are, in fact, promoted. Others suggest that the method does not promote those values and beliefs essential to our way of life. While the process emphasizes both rational thinking and emotional awareness in any examination of behavior patterns, it clearly fails to promote even a rudimentary commitment to the civic values which lie at the heart of our constitutional democracy.

As envisioned by Raths, Harmin, and Simon (1978), the process consists of seven steps:

1. Choosing freely
2. Choosing from alternatives
3. Choosing after thoughtful consideration of the consequences of each alternative
4. Prizing and cherishing
5. Affirming
6. Acting upon choices
7. Repeating

In spite of middle grades students' need for developing a coherent and consistent set of values, particularly those contained in the political documents (e.g., U.S. Constitution, Declaration of Independence, and Bill of Rights) that frame the values, beliefs, and ethical principles to which this nation adheres, there are numerous naive educators opposed to any overt involvement of students with value-related issues. Efforts to protect students from serious value-related issues are counterproductive, as this forces them to look elsewhere for answers to serious questions.

As Simon, Howe, and Kirschenbaum (1972) put it, their position is twofold. First, they are committed to teaching a set of core values, those that define the United States of America as a social, political, economic, and moral entity in the family of nations. Second, they are convinced that people learn best when they internalize what they live, when schools and schooling are more democratic in their structure and function, and when students learn how to value before they assess and embrace a functional set of values from among the multitude of competing value perspectives.

Although the use of values clarification declined in the 1980s, many educators still use many of the strategies associated with this form of values education. Kirschenbaum (1992), one of the early proponents of values clarification, attributes this decline to "changing times, faddism, stagnation, erratic implementation, and a major flaw in the theory of values clarification itself" (p. 773). This major flaw, according to Kirschenbaum (1992), is the insistence by proponents of values clarification "that [it] by itself [is] a sufficient method for developing satisfying values and moral behavior in young people" (p. 774). The benefit of values clarification is its focus on providing students with the necessary skills to make reasoned value choices. However, some degree of inculcation and modeling is a necessary adjunct to the method. There is value in both the traditional and new approaches to both value education and moral education.

SOCIAL STUDIES AND THE TEACHING OF VALUES

In recent years, school personnel, parents, and the general public have engaged in debate and discussion regarding what values schools ought to teach (Apple & Beane, 1995). Terms like *character education, value training, moral education, transmission of cultural values,* and *socialization* all have appeared in the national debate. People from all walks of life, reflecting myriad moral and ethical perspectives, seem to agree that the moral fiber of our society has deteriorated. Growing inequality and poverty, an erosion of family values, a decline in respect for authority, sex and violence on television, a rise in gang involvement among youth—all these are examples of such deterioration. Such examples serve to fuel the national debate.

Entire educational journals are devoted to character education (e.g., *Educational Leadership,* 1993). The Character Education Partnership was launched in March 1993 as a national coalition committed to placing character development at the forefront of the nation's educational agenda (Lickona, 1993).

Defining the Terms

In any discussion, participants ought to share a common understanding of the terms that frame the discussion. Such agreement is essential in any discussion of the role of public schools in the moral and character education of youth. Ryan (Center for the Advancement of Ethics and Character, Boston University) defines several terms commonly used in the character education debate as follows: *Moral* refers to the rightness or wrongness of something based on what a community believes to be good or right in conduct or character; *ethical* refers to more universal standards and codes of moral principles; *values* refers to what we desire, a sense of feeling about things; *virtue* refers to general moral excellence or right action and thinking, but also to specific moral qualities, such as generosity or courage; *character* refers to someone's moral constitution or a cluster of virtues. Though such terms are defined in different ways (e.g., *A Dictionary of the Social Science, 1964*), Ryan's definitions are generally acceptable in the character education community. Thus they provide the operational definitions of this segment.

Proponents of character education exert pressure on local schools to teach morals. This is a concern with a long history (e.g., Aristotle, the Founding Fathers, Horace Mann, John Dewey). The public's perception of a decline in moral values is reflected in concerns about a lack of discipline in everyday life, pervasive drug use, and an increase in violence in schools, as evidenced in recent Gallup surveys (1991, 1992, 1993). Critics argue that schools either do not teach moral principles and values, or they teach values that conflict with the critics' own. Teachers, by contrast, argue that the schools have always taught moral principles and values, if not directly, certainly through the so-called hidden curriculum.

Much of the criticism that surrounds the teaching of ethical principles is due to the confusion between the personal and public spheres, as well as that between religious and secular values. The argument that it is both the historic and proper function of public schools to teach the ethical principles (see Table 2-1) which are the foundation of our constitutional democracy is compelling (Butts, 1988). A principal mission of public education has been and remains citizenship education (Allen & Stevens, 1994; Barr, Barth, & Shermis, 1977; Butts, 1988). Logically, then, it follows that the ethical principles schools promote

TABLE 2-1 The Rights and Obligations of Citizenship

Obligations	Rights
Justice	Freedom
Equality	Diversity
Authority	Privacy
Participation	Due process
Truth	Property
Patriotism	Human rights

Source: Adapted from R. Freeman Butts, *The Morality of Democratic Citizenship: Goals for Civic Education in the Republic's Third Century* (Calabasas, CA: Center for Civic Education, 1988), p. 136.

ought to be consistent with those embodied in the Declaration of Independence, the U.S. Constitution (Lutz, 1987), and its interpretation as reflected in U.S. Supreme Court decisions.

Guiding Values in Our Sociopolitical Context

Three ethical principles from Utilitarian philosophy—the philosophical foundation, in part, underpinning the nation's Founding Documents—are respect for persons, beneficence, and justice. These principles are fundamental to grappling with moral issues (*The Belmont Report*, 1978). Just as the same ethical principles are applied in medical circles, so too they may be applied to public education.

Respect for Persons
This principle implies that individuals should be treated as autonomous agents and that persons with diminished autonomy are entitled to protection. Children, the handicapped (in some cases), and the infirm are all persons with diminished autonomy. Four important rules follow this concept (Levine, 1987, p. 8).

1. *Informed Consent:* Students and parents can make responsible decisions only when they have all the information. They need to know the consequences of decisions regarding course selection, discipline procedures, academic placement, and behavior contracts. School officials must provide all necessary information to both respect and support students in the decision-making process.

2. *Truth-telling:* Often students approach teachers with serious personal problems such as abuse, sexual harassment, or peer difficulties. If a second or third party must be informed, as in the case of child abuse, the student needs to be told what will be done with the information.

3. *Confidentiality:* Although it is true there are situations that require reporting, in most cases student confidence should be maintained. Although student grades should be confidential, it is the individual's prerogative to share such information with others.

4. *Privacy:* Students have a right to keep their personal belongings private unless "sufficient cause" exists to require a search by school or law enforcement officials. Not only are these moral rules embodied in various amendments to the U.S. Constitution, but they also provide standards for making daily decisions in classrooms.

Beneficence
The medical profession views this as the most basic ethical principle. The Hippocratic Oath reflects it in this manner. "I will keep them from harm and injustice" (Levine, 1987, p. 9). Again, four operational rules follow:

1. One ought not inflict evil or harm.
2. One ought to prevent evil or harm.
3. One ought to remove evil or harm.
4. One ought to promote good.

Such rules provide a positive model for classroom management. Not only do they afford students protection, and respect for the individual, a classroom organized around such rules is consistent with the principles of a democratic society.

Justice

This principle is based on what is fair or deserved. Equals ought to be treated equally, thus expanding the concept of individual rights and responsibility. Individual rights, a core value in American society, is the foundation of our legal system. That individual responsibility is the flip side of such rights is axiomatic, or should be!

Butts (1988) cites 12 values that are important to teach students. He divides this list into two areas: the obligations of citizenship and the rights of citizenship (see Table 2-1). Since there can be no rights without concomitant responsibilities, it is this juxtaposition we need to help students understand and incorporate into both their vision of active and responsible citizenship and their personal behavior patterns.

The Role of Social Studies

Although the entire school program ought to reflect a clear commitment to promoting the values of civism, the social studies fills a unique role in educating for active and responsible citizenship. For it is only in social studies curriculum that knowledge, skills, values, and commitment to participation blend into a concerted program of citizenship education. As an "integration of experience and knowledge concerning human relations for the purpose of citizenship education" (Barr, Barth, & Shermis, 1977), social studies offers students the opportunity to become good citizens. Sadly, the reality is much less positive. In fact, much of what passes for social studies curriculum and instruction is designed to promote good citizenship in a rather narrow sense (Barr, Barth, & Shermis, 1977).

SOCIAL PARTICIPATION

Middle grades students are citizens and ought to have every opportunity for active involvement in the local community. As citizens, they can contribute to community life in numerous ways and should be encouraged to move beyond merely discussing important issues to becoming involved in them at the local level.

Opportunities for involvement in the community that promote intellectual development, an appreciation for the role of citizens in a democratic society, and active and responsible citizenship abound. A description of two participatory programs (CAAP and Service Learning) is provided in Chapter 4.

Participatory activities need to be carefully structured to allow students to:

1. Perform tasks that both students and the community consider worthwhile
2. Take responsibility for making decisions within community-based projects or placements
3. Place themselves in positions of responsibility in which others depend on their actions
4. Work on tasks that challenge and strengthen their thinking, both cognitively and ethically
5. Work with peers and adults on group efforts toward common goals
6. Reflect systematically on their community experience

Middle grades students face a myriad of social and personal problems that are directly related to the developmental realities of early adolescence. In learning to cope with attendant physical, social, emotional, and intellectual growth processes, early adolescents need to address a plethora of real and practical problems on a regular, recurring basis in their educational experience. This is possible through participation in various public and private community agencies, community projects, social and political action activities, and internship experiences (see Chapter 4 for two examples of such programs).

The following serve as examples of projects involving middle grades students in the local community:

1. *Neighborhood Help Clubs.* These clubs assist people in a given neighborhood or rural area (e.g., elderly, disabled) in performing essential tasks that they are unable to complete on their own.
2. *Environmental Cleanup Day.* A day is designated for a cleanup experience around the school, neighborhood, or entire local community.
3. *Direct Community Involvement Experiences.* A day is spent in a court of law, in a police station, riding or walking the "beat" with a police officer, and in active involvement in areas of community concern (e.g., local election center, city hall, sewage treatment plant).
4. *Long-Range Involvement Projects.* A long-range plan of involvement with a people-oriented community organization such as a home for the elderly, a hospital, or the American Red Cross is developed and executed.
5. *Field Trips.* Trips are planned that are on-site and include direct research, observation, and data collection relevant to a particular topic.

6. *Direct Action Projects.* Projects designed to promote the well-being of specific groups (e.g., UNICEF, CROP Walk, walk-a-thons and bike-a-thons for specific organizations) are developed, initiated, and carried out (Allen, 1980).

7. *Learn–Serve.* Projects that are school- and/or community-based (MacNichol, 1993).

Finally, any time "different" learning experiences are provided for students, it is important to plan and execute them carefully. The following guidelines, based on those developed by Banks and Clegg (1977), are useful in developing and implementing projects of this nature:

1. Community involvement projects should provide opportunities for students to develop a strong sense of political efficacy.
2. An essential prerequisite to community involvement is a careful study of the issue.
3. It is essential to secure the cooperation of teachers, administrators, parents, and concerned community leaders prior to implementing involvement projects.
4. The middle school environment and schedule should be conducive to such projects.
5. Students should be made fully aware of the possible consequences of their potential action.
6. Community involvement should be meaningful to those taking part. It should relate to relevant personal and community concerns.

The need to provide appropriate social studies experiences beyond the classroom and outside the school building is great. In developing active and responsible citizens, direct, first-hand involvement in the local community is a superb way to lend the degree of "realness" so essential to promoting commitment to democratic processes. Such programs for grades 5 to 8 are offered by the Close Up Foundation, the Civic Achievement Aware Program (CAAP), and CAAP in Action: The Environment. They provide excellent avenues for promoting active and responsible citizenship. CAAP is described in Chapter 4.

THE MIDDLE-LEVEL CONNECTION: QUESTIONS TO PONDER

For Preservice Students
1. Describe your middle grades social studies experiences.
2. Are there parallels between your middle grades social studies experiences and those of your peers?

3. How do your middle grades social studies experiences compare or contrast with your developing understanding of the nature of "good" middle grades teaching practices?
4. Describe the principal instructional methods you think you will employ in teaching social studies. Why do you think you may teach in the manner described?
5. How does your definition of social studies compare to the one that is offered in this chapter? Discuss any similarities or differences.
6. Do you agree that the central goal of social studies should be citizenship education? Explain your response.
7. What is your position on the need to promote commitment to rational processes as the central means of resolving problems, making decisions, and determining positions on critical issues?
8. During your middle grades social studies experiences, did you ever engage in community-based, social-action activities? If yes, explain the involvement. If no, what are your thoughts on requiring such activity as part of social studies at the middle grades level?

For Inservice Students
1. What were your social studies experiences like when you were in the middle grades?
2. Are there parallels between your middle-level social studies experiences and those of your students?
3. Which social studies tradition most closely approximates your philosophical perspective?
4. What degree of consistency exists between your perspective on instruction and the actual classroom practices through which you engage students in the study of social sciences?
5. Describe the social studies content for which you are responsible. How does it compare to the content taught at other grade levels?
6. Is your social studies curriculum interdisciplinary or integrated with other components of the core curriculum in any way? Explain your response.
7. Do you make a concerted effort to integrate social studies with other components of the core curriculum? Explain your responses.
8. Describe the principal instructional method you employ in social studies (reflective/nonreflective) and the instructional techniques that predominate in your classes.
9. React to the social studies definition presented in this chapter. How does it compare to your definition?
10. Do you agree that the central goal for social studies is or should be citizenship education? Why? If not, what should be the goal?

11. Does the knowledge base of your social studies program incorporate the social sciences, humanities, and students' personal life experiences? Explain your response.
12. What skills are taught in your social studies program? How are they learned and practiced?
13. Is your social studies skills program sequential, and are the skills taught in a systematic manner?
14. What values and beliefs lie at the heart of your social studies program? How do these compare to those in your school's so-called hidden curriculum?
15. To what extent does your social studies program promote commitment to rational processes as the central means to resolve problems, make decisions, and otherwise determine positions on critical issues?
16. Do you provide students with opportunities to engage in developmentally appropriate community-based social-action activities as part of the social studies curriculum? If not, why?
17. Describe the ways in which your students are actively and responsibly engaged in the local community and related social-action activities.

Take the time to discuss your responses with colleagues and others interested in taking a hard look at your school's social studies curriculum. Ask your students how they feel about social studies. Furthermore, ask them what type of social studies experiences they believe will promote a more active and responsible citizenship.

FOOD FOR THOUGHT BEFORE MOVING ON

1. When was the last time you seriously reflected on your philosophy of education? Do you find thinking about your educational philosophy has an influence on your teaching behavior?
2. How often do you take the time to ascertain the degree of consistency between what you believe about teaching and learning and your pedagogical behavior in the classroom?
3. What professional development activities do you engage in to expand your social studies knowledge base?
4. How do you remain current on social studies?
5. How often do you personally become actively involved in the local community?
6. To what extent do your administrators support your professional development and need to remain current?

REFERENCES

Allen, Michael G. (1980). "Social Studies Call for Social Action." *Middle School Journal, 11*(4):13–14.

Allen, Michael, and Robert Stevens. (1994). *Middle grades social studies: teaching for active and responsible citizenship,* 1st ed. Boston: Allyn and Bacon.

Apple, Michael, and James Beane, eds. (1995). *Democratic Schools.* Alexandria, VA: Association for Supervision and Curriculum Development.

Banks, James A., and Ambrose Clegg. (1977). *Teaching Strategies for the Social Studies: Inquiry, Valuing, and Decision-Making.* Menlo Park, CA: Addison-Wesley.

Barr, Robert D., James Barth, and S. Samuel Shermis. (1977). *Defining the Social Studies.* Bulletin No. 51. Washington, DC: National Council for the Social Studies.

Bragaw, Donald, and H. Michael Hartoonian. (1988). "Social Studies: The Study of People in Society." In Ronald Brandt, ed., *Content of the Curriculum, 1988 Yearbook.* Alexandria, VA: Association for Supervision and Curriculum Development.

Building a History Curriculum: Guidelines for Teaching History in Schools. (1988). Prepared by the Bradley Commission on History in the Schools. Washington, DC: Educational Excellence Network.

Butts, R. Freeman. (1988). *Morality of Democratic Citizenship: Goals for Civic Education in the Third Century.* Calabasas, CA: Center for Civic Education, p. 136.

Cassidy, E., and D. Kurfman. (1977). "Decision Making as Purpose and Process." In D. Kurfman, ed., *Developing Decision-Making Skills. 47th Yearbook.* Arlington, VA: National Council for the Social Studies.

Chapin, James, and Richard Gross. (1963). *Teaching Social Studies Skills.* Boston: Little, Brown.

Charting a Course: Social Studies for the 21st Century. (1989). Washington, DC: National Commission on Social Studies in the Schools.

Checkley, Kathy. (1996). *Geography's Renaissance: Restoring Earth to the K–12 Curriculum.* Curriculum update. Alexandria, VA: Association for Supervision and Curriculum Development.

Commager, Henry, and Raymond Muessig. (1980). *The Study and Teaching of History.* Columbus, OH: Merrill.

Curwin, Richard, and C. Curwin. (1974). *Developing Individual Values in the Classroom.* Palo Alto, CA: Learning Handbooks.

Daniels, Richard. (1972). *Studying History: How and Why,* 2nd ed. Englewood Cliffs, NJ: Prentice Hall.

Educational Leadership. (1993). *51*(3). Entire issue devoted to character education.

Gould, Julius, and William Kolb, eds. (1964). *A Dictionary of the Social Sciences*. New York: The Free Press.

Guidelines for Geographic Education: Elementary and Secondary Schools. (1984). Washington, DC: Joint Committee of the National Council for Geographic Education and Association of American Geographers.

Heilbroner, Richard. (1960). *The Future as History*. New York: Grove Press.

Hepburn, Mary, ed. (1983). *Democratic Education in the Schools and Classrooms*. Bulletin No. 70. Washington, DC: National Council for the Social Studies.

Howe, L., and M. Howe. (1975). *Personalizing Education: Values Clarification and Beyond*. New York: Hart.

"In Search of a Scope and Sequence for Social Studies: Report of the National Council for Social Studies Task Force on Scope and Sequence." (1989). *Social Education, 53*(6):386–387.

Joyce, Bruce. (1972). *New Strategies for Social Education*. Chicago: SRA.

Kirschenbaum, Howard. (1992). "A Comprehensive Model for Values Education and Moral Education." *Phi Delta Kappan*, 771–776.

Kitchens, James, and Raymond Muessig. (1980). *The Study and Teaching of Sociology*. Columbus, OH: Merrill.

Levine, Carol. (1987). *Taking Sides: Clashing Views on Controversial Bioethical Issues*, 2nd ed. Guilford, CT: Dushkin Publishing Group.

Lickona, Thomas. (1993). "The Return of Character Education." *Educational Leadership, 51*(3), 6–11.

Lounsbury, John, and J. Howard Johnston. (1988). *Life in the Three 6th Grades*. Reston, VA: National Association of Secondary School Principals.

Lutz, Donald. (1987). "The Origins of American Constitutionalism." In Claire Keller and Denny Schillings, eds., *Teaching about the Constitution*. Bulletin #80. Washington, DC: National Council for the Social Studies, pp. 3–11.

MacNichol, Roland. (1983). "Service Learning: A Challenge to Do the Right Thing." *Equity and Excellence in Education*, 26(2):9–11.

Manson, Gary, and Merrill Ridd, eds. (1977). *New Perspectives on Geographic Education: Putting Theory into Practice*. Dubuque, IA: Kendall/Hunt.

Miller, James, and Jon Young. (1979). "Social Studies as Personal Development." *The North Carolina Journal for the Social Studies*, 1–7.

National Geography Standards: Geography for Life. (1994). Geography Education Standards Project, American Geographical Society, Association of American Geographers, National Council for Geographic Education, and National Geographic Society.

Parker, Walter, and John Jarolimek. (1984). *Citizenship and the Critical Role of the Social Studies*. Bulletin No. 72. Washington, DC: National Council for the Social Studies. Boulder, CO: Social Science Education Consortium.

Pelto, Paul, and Raymond Muessig. (1980). *The Study and Teaching of Anthropology*. Columbus, OH: Merrill.

Raths, Louis, Merrill Harmin, and Sidney Simon. (1978). *Values and Teaching,* 2nd ed. Columbus, OH: Merrill.

Ryan, Kevin. (1994). Used by permission of the author.

Selwyn, Douglas. (1995). *Art and Humanities in the Social Studies.* Bulletin No. 90. Washington, DC: National Council for the Social Studies.

Simon, Sidney, L. Howe, and H. Kirschenbaum. (1972). *Values Clarification: A Handbook of Practical Strategies for Teachers and Students.* New York: Hart.

Smith, John A., Jay A. Monson, and Dorothy Dobson. (1992). "A Case Study on Integrating History and Reading Instruction through Literature." *Social Education, 56*(7): 370–375.

"Social Studies in the Middle School: A Report of the Task Force on Social Studies in the Middle School." (1991). *Social Education, 55*(5):287–293.

Straayer, John. (1980). *The Study and Teaching of Political Science.* Columbus, OH: Merrill.

Superka, Douglas. (1974). "Approaches to Values Education." *Social Science Newsletter,* No. 20.

Teaching with Documents: Using Primary Sources from the National Archives. (1989). Washington, DC: National Archives and Records Administration.

The Twenty-first Annual Gallup Poll of the Public's Attitude toward Public Schools. (1991). *Phi Delta Kappan, 73*(1), 55.

The Twenty-second Annual Gallup Poll of the Public's Attitude toward Public Schools. (1992). *Phi Delta Kappan, 74*(1), 43.

The Twenty-third Annual Gallup Poll of the Public's Attitude toward Public Schools. (1993). *Phi Delta Kappan, 75*(2), 139.

Volkmer, Carl, Anne L. Pasanella, and Louis E. Raths. (1977). *Values in the Classroom.* Columbus, OH: Merrill.

Warmke, Robert, and Raymond Muessig. (1980). *The Study and Teaching of Economics.* Columbus, OH: Merrill.

3

EARLY ADOLESCENCE: A TIME OF CHANGE AND TRANSITION

An effective middle-level education program must take into consideration the nature of the student population. Some of the most significant changes in life occur during early adolescence, which generally covers ages 10 to 15.

Far-reaching changes in physical, social, emotional, and intellectual characteristics take place with surprising rapidity. An educational structure that does not account for such dramatic changes is simply not fulfilling its obligations to recognize and accommodate the whole person.

It is important, then, to understand more fully the unique developmental characteristics of this age group before planning or redesigning social studies programs that promote a commitment to active and responsible citizenship (Thornburg, 1973, 1980).

CONCEPTUAL NECESSITIES

Attention to the developmental characteristics and related educational needs of early adolescents is a hallmark of good middle-level schools, which in fact address these aspects of development in quite specific and concrete ways (Garvin, 1989; Georgiady & Romano, 1977).

Early adolescence as a definable period of human growth and development received increased attention in the 1980s. This recent focus has occurred for a number of reasons. New and continuing research on human development has added significantly to our knowledge base of the characteristics of this age group. Furthermore, the cyclical interest in educational programming as associated with cognitive development is currently enjoying a renaissance in the public at large. Finally, the multitude of personal, family, emotional, and social problems exhibited by this age group has caught the attention of both educators and the general public (Eichhorn, 1984; Johnston & Markle, 1986; Carnegie Council, 1989; Johnston, 1990).

The need to focus more attention on early adolescents as they negotiate the transition from childhood to young adulthood must be recognized by all those responsible for their welfare. Educators and others responsible for planning educational programs for these youths must be a part of such a focus.

What, then, are the developmental characteristics of early adolescence? What makes these young people so unique and, apparently, in need of a particular type of educational experience? Finally, what is the potential impact of such development on the social studies components of schooling ("Social Studies in the Middle School," 1991; Thornburg, 1981)?

If we view human development as a continuous process, it is evident that no clearly delineated events characterize entrance into or exit from the developmental period called early adolescence. Early adolescents are identified by such terms, among others, as *transescents, emerging adolescents, preadolescents, young adolescents*, and *in-betweeners.*

The typical age range of early adolescence is 10 or 11 to 14 or 15. It is recognized that overlap exists at each end of the range. Early adolescent growth is usually viewed from four developmental perspectives—physical, social, emotional, and intellectual.

Physical Development

Early adolescence is characterized by periods of pronounced and accelerated physical growth marked by increasing height, muscular strength, and the development of primary sexual characteristics in both males and females. Growth patterns make this period of development unique in the human life cycle.

Among the early adolescent population, annual weight gain averages 8 to 10 pounds. Height increases, on average, 2 inches. Females are usually taller and more physically advanced than males. In males, bone growth surpasses muscle development with a concomitant lack of protection of both bones and tendons; hence, the ungainliness and lack of coordination of males in this age group.

Variations in metabolic rates result in extreme restlessness and alternating periods of hyperactivity and fatigue. Ossification of cartilage in epiphysial areas of the skeleton make sitting on hard surfaces or for a long time extremely difficult. This reality calls for individual and small-group instructional techniques that provide opportunities for movement within the classroom, rather than lectures or a large group recitation format. These and related physical characteristics of early adolescence are presented in Figure 3-1.

In addition to the many direct effects physical diversity has on early adolescents, other areas of development, such as social and emotional factors, are significantly influenced by circumstances that relate to early or late physical development.

The results of such diverse physical development differ greatly from person to person. Each individual establishes unique trademarks, idiosyncrasies, and peculiarities, while developing many commonalities, tendencies, and needs typical of those of peers (Mitchell, 1974, 1979).

With the possible exception of infancy, no other time rivals early adolescence in the degree of growth occurring or brings about such physical changes and problems. Educators knowledgeable about the physical metamorphosis that occurs during early adolescence are better able to establish goals and plan appropriate social studies programs for middle grades students.

---

1. Physical development is reflected in increasing height, body breadth and depth, heart size, lung capacity, muscular strength, and sexual development.
2. Average annual weight gain is 8 to 10 pounds; in height, 2 inches. Girls are usually taller and more physically advanced than boys.
3. Bone growth surpasses muscle development; bones lack protection of muscles and support of tendons. This uneven bone-muscle growth facilitates physical regression in poor coordination and poor body mechanics.
4. Sexual maturation is closely related to general physical development. Examples include the growth of genitalia in boys and breast development in girls.
5. Extreme restlessness and alternating periods of almost hyperactivity and fatigue reflect variations in metabolic rates. Daily needs for release of energy and periods in which wide variations in blood sugar stability require nutritional breaks characterize early adolescence. Overexertion may result in chronic fatigue. Ossification of cartilage in epiphysial areas of the skeleton makes sitting on hardsurfaced chairs extremely uncomfortable and is one of the reasons for the "ants-in-the-pants," "can't-sit-still" problems of this age.
6. Overtaxing the digestive system with large quantities of poorly selected foods is a normal experimental activity of this age.
7. Concern with appearance reflects peer and "pop" fads created by various media.

FIGURE 3-1 Physical Characteristics of Early Adolescence

Adapted from *This We Believe.* (1982, 1992). Columbus, OH: National Middle School Association. Used with permission.

Social Development

Early adolescents leave the comparative serenity of childhood behind, as they broaden their base of affiliation from family to the peer group. Their desire for social acceptance leads to attempts to become, in effect, gregarious. Often, individuality is sacrificed in a desire to be accepted by the peer group.

Not infrequently, group loyalty entails indifference or cruelty to outsiders (Thornburg & Gould, 1980). Such conformity may often run counter to adult expectations. Although early adolescents exhibit a continuing need for identification with adults, they often reject adults' suggestions in their desire for independence. These and related social characteristics are presented in Figure 3-2.

Feelings about parents, teachers, friends, peers, and others undergo significant change during early adolescence. Interpersonal relationships take on new dimensions and indicate changing personal perspectives on the part of young adolescents. This new perspective includes the recognition that even the most trusted adults are not perfect and may not always be dependable.

---

1. Early adolescents broaden their base of affiliation from family to peer group.
2. The desire for social acceptance leads to attempts to become effectively gregarious. Individuality is surrendered in a desire to be accepted. While heterosexual relations grow, same sex affiliations dominate. Rapid shifts in interest develop along with striking individual differences.
3. Group loyalty carries out group will with indifference and sometimes cruelty to outsiders. Conformity to the group in terms of mannerisms, dress, speech, and behavior often run counter to social expectations of adults.
4. Early adolescents vacillate between the desire for regulation and direction and their demand for independence. They have a continuing need for identification with adults but reserve the right to accept or reject adults' suggestions.
5. Early adolescents are willing to work hard and sacrifice, especially if social rewards are involved. Altruism and high ideals in the search for beauty and truth are directed toward institutions such as schools, community, church, and government.

FIGURE 3-2   Social Characteristics of Early Adolescence

Adapted from *This We Believe* (1982, 1992). Columbus, OH: National Middle School Association. Used with permission.

Emotional Development

Closely related to social development, the emotional developmental changes experienced by early adolescents are no less profound (see Figure 3-3). Such changes relate to adjustment to personal growth patterns and relationships with adults. Both social and emotional changes are affected by the physical changes that take place during this time.

There comes a point during early adolescence when youths begin to understand the need for more balanced views. Until then, they are beset with internal conflicts and often exhibit a mixture of anxiety and bravado.

1. These characteristics relate to adjustment to personal growth patterns and relationships with adults.

2. Early adolescents must begin to deal with and to understand "shades of gray" as opposed to "black and white" choices. They are beset with internal conflicts to which they respond with variations of anxiety and fear, reassuring bravado, shyness, and noisiness. They test the psychological confines of the adult value system.

3. Early adolescents tend to make exaggerated responses to anything with sexual implications. One's sexual development is subject to comparison with peer and media expectations, not only of body change but personal habits and practices. The need to sort fact from folklore is a continuing emotional challenge to the early adolescent.

4. Early adolescents desire attention, at times without regard to how it is secured. Threats and release of tension through emotional outbursts are episodic reflections of rapid shifts and variations of mood.

5. Instances of expressed or implied criticism from adult sources are not easily tolerated. Strong desires to move toward increasing levels of independence and personal decision making contrast with felt needs for the security of adult reassurance and direction.

6. Adult standards and conventions may be ignored, ridiculed, and, at times, defied at the level of family authority. Once desirous of pleasing parents and teachers, early adolescents often become rebellious toward adults. They tend to be easily offended and ready to believe that adults do not understand them. Often inconsiderate of others, they may monopolize the family's telephone, television, bathroom, and magazines.

FIGURE 3-3   Emotional Characteristics of Early Adolescence

Adapted from *This We Believe* (1982, 1992). Columbus, OH: National Middle School Association. Used with permission.

Early adolescents tend to make exaggerated responses to anything that has sexual implications. They also desire attention, often without regard to the feelings of others, and they often rebel against adult standards and conventions. Variability in behavior reflects rapid shifts in mood.

Early adolescents are also searching for self-identity amid a plethora of sex role models, a changing social and emotional environment, and the impact of physical development on their day-to-day functioning. They experience exceptionally turbulent emotions, and there is a tremendous flexibility in self-concept during this period (Beane & Lipka, 1987; Hoffman, 1980; James, 1980).

Conscience becomes more apparent during early adolescence. Intense feelings about fairness, honesty, and other values characterize the period. Morality is based more on what has been absorbed from the culture of the age group than on thoughtful meditation or reflection. The conscience is more pragmatic than ideal and more egocentric than altruistic. A primary goal during this time is to learn the skills that bring recognition and gain esteem from peers.

Intellectual Development

During early adolescence, most youths operate within Piaget's concrete and formal stages of thought (Inhelder & Piaget, 1958). Numerous studies indicate that virtually all children acquire concrete operations, although many adults never attain the formal operations stage. During this transition, mental operations are not consistent and may vary according to the nature of the tasks attempted (see Figure 3-4).

Studies indicate that most early adolescents operate at the concrete level. Despite findings (Hallman, 1969) that most early adolescents under the age of 16.2 reason at the concrete level, many teachers continue to expect them to operate at the formal level.

Such variability, which seems to occur especially when subject content is unfamiliar and abstract (Sinnott, 1975), should be an important consideration for middle grades social studies programs. Toepfer reports, for example, that "the synthesis of available findings shows that no more than one percent of 10 year olds, five percent of 11 year olds, twelve percent of 12 year olds, fourteen percent of 13 year olds, and fourteen percent of 14 year olds have the capacity to even initiate formal operations" (Toepfer, 1980, p. 226).

Students who reach the formal stage of thought begin to think with greater logic and consistency but are novices compared to those in later stages of development. Mitchell offers insight into the cognitive process when he states that "for the most part, early adolescents are exempt from thinking extensively about the larger issues such as government, race, or religion and when they do think about these issues the reflections are essen-

1. Early adolescents are able to initiate new and higher cognitive processing due to brain growth.
2. Early adolescents are intensely curious.
3. Early adolescents enjoy both manipulative and intellectually stimulating learning experiences, including active involvement rather than passive recipiency.
4. Early adolescents are generally intellectually uninhibited and find learning most interesting when it is related to immediate goals and interests.
5. Early adolescents express a heightened egocentricism. They argue to clarify personal thinking as much as to convince others.
6. Early adolescents exhibit strong desires for self-expression and preferences for creative activity.
7. Early adolescents exhibit a growing interest in transposing self and others into other situations.
8. Early adolescents display wide ranges of skills, interests, and abilities. Interests, attention span, and concentration alter during this period of growth and result generally in shorter rather than longer periods of focus.
9. In their search for identity, early adolescents seek to understand the meaning and enigmas of life from many perspectives.
10. Early adolescents are concerned with intellectual, philosophical, biological, sociological, moral, and ethical issues. They seek causal and correlative relationships.

FIGURE 3-4   Intellectual Characteristics of Early Adolescence

Adapted from *This We Believe* (1982, 1992). Columbus, OH: National Middle School Association. Used with permission.

tially personal and immediate rather than abstract and general" (Mitchell, 1979, p. 20).

Some educators believe more abstract subject matter should be initiated in order to promote and speed up the attainment of formal operations. Research by Kuhn (1979) and others, however, demonstrates that efforts to speed this transition to formal thinking is largely unsuccessful. Brown (1982) notes that Piaget's own view was that such development takes much time and, therefore, is a long-term goal. It is not a matter of "how fast we can help intelligence grow but how far we can help it grow" (Duckworth, 1979, p. 303).

Research on brain periodization suggests that there may be a biological basis for stages of cognitive development. Research studies indicate that many children between the ages of 12 to 14 years are in a period of minimal brain growth. It has been theorized that, during these nongrowth periods, early adolescents should not be expected to develop new cognitive skills (Toepfer, 1980). However, research continues in this important area of human development.

Clearly, many members of this age group remain limited in their reasoning ability to understand immediate or past events and have difficulty with problems that contain more than two simultaneous dimensions or relations. Others, however, have negotiated the transition between the real and the impossible and are able to hypothesize contrary-to-fact possibilities (Baumrind, 1978). As in other areas of early adolescence, wide diversity exists in intellectual development and must be considered when social studies programs are designed.

Conclusion

Probably less is known about early adolescence than any other period of human development. Relatively little is known about the changing interactions of these youths with their families, schools, peers, or communities (Lipsitz, 1980). Knowledge is increasing, however, and concerted efforts must be made to use such knowledge in promoting a commitment to active and responsible citizenship.

Early adolescence must be viewed as more than just a period of transition. As Lipsitz (1980) wrote, "to see adolescence so exclusively as a transitional stage is to deny it the integrity we grant other stages of life" (p. 22). This label, if literally defined, may serve as a barrier against concentrated attempts to provide a more complete and accurate understanding of early adolescence. It is a pivotal time during which many basic attitudes and behaviors are formed that will remain dominant for a lifetime.

This period is one in which a large number of these youths will experience stress and other difficulties (Carnegie Council, 1989). In spite of this reality, early adolescence is a time of new and exciting possibilities. It is also filled with many pleasures, as physical growth offers many novel and intriguing experiences; as intellectual growth allows a more comprehensive view of the world; as social growth unveils the excitement of new peer relationships and new views of comradeship; and as psychological growth allows the emergence of the recognition of self as a primary person, not simply a reflection of the expectations of parents, teachers, and society (Mitchell, 1979).

THE SOCIAL STUDIES CONNECTION: QUESTIONS TO PONDER

For Preservice Students
1. What do you remember about your early adolescent years? Briefly describe an event in your middle grades years that captures the essence of the developmental realities of that stage.

2. Has your understanding of early adolescence changed as a result of reading this chapter? In what ways?
3. What we now know about early adolescent intellectual development suggests that it is entirely appropriate to raise our expectations of their cognitive performance. Do you agree or disagree? Explain your response.
4. Early adolescent developmental characteristics call for active involvement in meaningful social studies activities that enable students to make logical connections to life realities. Do you agree or disagree? Explain your response.
5. The transitional nature of early adolescence calls for concentrating less on content and more on instruction in skill development. Do you agree or disagree? Explain your response.

For Inservice Students
1. What do you remember about your early adolescent years? Briefly describe an event in your middle grades years that captures the essence of the developmental realities of that stage.
2. How have you kept pace with the explosion of recent knowledge on early adolescence? Be specific.
3. Has your thinking on early adolescence changed as a result of this new knowledge? In what way?
4. Has your response toward early adolescents changed as you have learned more about the age group? Describe any specific changes in your pedagogical practices?
5. Have any of your teaching techniques changed as a result of this increased knowledge base? Describe briefly.
6. Do your pedagogical practices and general classroom expectations of early adolescents consider the following:
   Physical developmental realities of early adolescence? How?
   Social developmental realities of early adolescence? How?
   Emotional developmental realities of early adolescence? How?
   Intellectual developmental realities of early adolescence? How?
7. Brain periodization research notwithstanding, what we now know about early adolescence suggests that it is entirely appropriate to raise our expectations of young adolescents' cognitive performance. Do you agree or disagree? Explain your response.
8. Early adolescent developmental characteristics call for active involvement in meaningful social studies activities that enable students to make logical connections to life realities. Do you agree or disagree? Explain your response.
9. If you agree with the premise in Question 8, in what ways do you incorporate it into the social studies curriculum or otherwise promote active learning?

10. In what ways do you tailor your instructional practices and skill development strategies in social studies to this age group?

Take the time to discuss your responses with colleagues and others interested in taking a hard look at your school's social studies curriculum. Ask your students what they know about the developmental realities they are experiencing. Also, ask them how you might all take advantage of this time of transition to foster more active and responsible citizenship on their part.

FOOD FOR THOUGHT BEFORE MOVING ON

1. When did you last engage in serious reading about early adolescence?
2. Have you taken time to reflect on the educational implications of early adolescent development?
3. What professional development activities do you engage in to expand your knowledge base of the educational implications of early adolescent development?
4. How do you remain current on understanding the social, emotional, and intellectual changes in your students?
5. How often do you play an active, supportive, enhancing role in the out-of-class lives of your students?
6. To what extent do(es) your building administrator(s) support your professional development and need to remain current on early adolescent development and the related educational implications of such information? What can be done to foster further support?

REFERENCES

Baumrind, Donald. (1978). "Perspectives and Recommendations for the Science Directorate." In *Early Adolescence: Perspectives and Recommendations*. Washington, DC: National Science Foundation.

Beane, James, and Richard Lipka. (1987). *When Kids Come First: Enhancing Self-Esteem*. Columbus, OH: National Middle School Association.

Brown, James. (1982). "Developmental Transition in the Middle School: Designing Strategies for Social Studies." In Linda Rosenzweig, ed., *Developmental Perspectives in the Social Studies*. Bulletin No. 66. Washington, DC: National Council for the Social Studies.

Carnegie Council on Adolescent Development. (1989). *Turning Points: Preparing American Youth for the 21st Century*. New York: Carnegie Corporation of New York.

Caught in the Middle: Educational Reform for Young Adolescents in California Public Schools. (1988). Middle Grades Task Force. Sacramento: California Department of Education.

Duckworth, E. (1979). "Either We're Too Costly and They Can't Learn or We're Too Late and They Know It Already: The Dilemma of Applying Piaget." *Harvard Educational Review, 49*(3):297–312.

Eichhorn, Donald. (1984). "The Nature of Transescents." In John Lounsbury, ed., *Perspectives: Middle School Education, 1964–1984.* Columbus, OH: National Middle School Association, pp. 30–38.

Garvin, James. (1989). *Learning How to Kiss a Frog.* Rowley, MA: New England League of Middle Schools.

Georgiady, Nicholas, and Louis Romano. (1977). "Growth Characteristics of Middle School Children: Curriculum Implications." *Middle School Journal, 7*(1):12–15, 22–23.

Hallman, R. (1969). "Piaget and the Teaching of History." *Educational Research, 12*:3–12.

Hoffman, M. (1980). "Fostering Moral Development." In M. Johnson, ed., *Toward Adolescence: The Middle School Years.* Chicago: National Society for the Study of Education Yearbook.

Inhelder, B., and Jean Piaget. (1958). *The Growth of Logical Thinking from Childhood to Adolescence.* New York: Basic Books.

James, M. (1980). "Early Adolescent Ego Development." *The High School Journal, 63*(6):244–249.

Johnston, J. Howard. (1990). *The New American Family and the School.* Columbus, OH: National Middle School Association.

Johnston, J. Howard, and Glenn C. Markle. (1986). *What Research Says to the Middle Level Practitioner.* Columbus, OH: National Middle School Association.

Lipsitz, Joan. (1980). "The Age Group." In M. Johnson, ed., *Toward Adolescence: The Middle School Years.* Chicago: National Society for the Study of Education Yearbook.

Kuhn, D. (1979). "The Application of Piaget's Theory of Cognitive Development to Education." *Harvard Educational Review, 49*(3):340–360.

Mitchell, John J. (1974). *Human Life: The Early Adolescent Years.* Toronto: Holt, Rinehart, and Winston.

Mitchell, John J. (1979). *Adolescent Psychology.* Toronto: Holt, Rinehart, and Winston.

Sinnott, J. (1975). "Everyday Thinking and Piagetian Operativity in Adults." *Human Development, 18*:430–443.

"Social Studies in the Middle School: A Report of the Task Force on Social Studies in the Middle School." (1991). *Social Education, 55*:287–293.

This We Believe. (1982, 1992). Columbus, OH: National Middle School Association.

Thornburg, Hershel. (1973). "Behaviors and Values: Consistency or Inconsistency." *Adolescence, 8*(32):503–510.

Thornburg, Hershel. (1980). "Can the Middle School Adapt to the Needs of Its Students?" In Edward Brazee and John Swaim, eds., *The Emerging Adolescent: Characteristics and Educational Implications.* Fairborn, OH: National Middle School Association.

Thornburg, Hershel. (1981). "Middle Level Social Studies: Curriculum Implications." *Contemporary Education, 52*(3):154–159.

Thornburg, Hershel, and A. Gould. (1980). *The Types of Peer Group Involvement in Middle School and Junior High School Students.* Paper presented to the Rocky Mountain Psychological Association, Denver, Colorado.

Toepfer, Conrad. (1980). "Brain Growth Periodization Data: Some Suggestions for Re-Thinking Middle Grades Education." *The High School Journal, 63*(6):222–227.

II

PRACTICE

CHAPTER 4
Social Studies Curriculum

CHAPTER 5
Instruction in Social Studies

CHAPTER 6
Critical Thinking Activities

In Part II, we invite the reader to consider the activity-based curriculum models that we present. We attempt to integrate theory with practice in a way that will provide many meaningful experiences for middle-level students. "Students should find most intrinsically fulfilling classwork that offers leeway for student initiative, creative expression, active participation in the learning activity, and social interaction with other learners, in keeping with the energy and desire to try out new abilities and associations at this age" (Braddock and McPartland, 1993). By participating in the proposed activities, students will begin to develop democratic attitudes and come to realize their responsibility as citizens.

Chapter 4 presents an overview of social studies curriculum. The need for middle schoolers to develop a sense of community participation and involvement is acute at their age. CAAP is one model that we believe is successful in achieving this end. Service-learning projects are another example.

Chapter 5 suggests several developmentally appropriate approaches to helping middle school students achieve skill development, learn content, and begin to assume citizenship responsibilities in a pluralistic society. Recent research in the areas of student-centered learning, critical thinking skills, writing skills, interdisciplinary activities, and cooperative learning is presented. The five geographic themes and Bloom's Taxonomy of Learning Objectives provide an organizing construct that will help students achieve a better understanding of the world and their place in it. In addition, four models of citizenship transmission, which show the evolution of democratic socialization and our position today, are offered.

Chapter 6 offers a variety of user-friendly activities that will engage middle-level students in critical thinking activities. The activities afford students opportunities that meet both their individual and group needs. Developmentally appropriate, the activities are suggestions that in-service and pre-service teachers can use in creating their own social studies lessons.

REFERENCE

Braddock, Jomills Henry, and James M. McPartland. (1993). "Education of Early Adolescents," *Review of Research in Education, 19.*

4

SOCIAL STUDIES CURRICULUM

SOCIAL STUDIES CURRICULUM EFFORTS

Efforts at social studies curriculum reform and setting national standards have been achieved in all areas of the social studies. This chapter provides examples in two areas: standards for social studies and national geography standards. Three activities—"Write a Local History," "Write Your Family History," and "People and Their Environment: Searching the Historical Record"—will demonstrate how the standards in social studies and geography can be met. Two additional examples of educational programs that focus on promoting active and responsible citizenship are the Service-Learning and Civic Achievement Award Program.

SOCIAL STUDIES CURRICULUM STANDARDS

"In 1992, the Board of Directors of the National Council for the Social Studies created a task force on Standards for the Social Studies in order to ensure that, in the 'era of standards,' an integrated social science, behavioral science, humanities approach for achieving academic and civic competence was available to guide social studies decision makers in K–12 schools in the United States" (p. xvii, Curriculum Standards for the Social Studies). The standards represent a national effort involving thousands of social studies educators. Teachers in the field, scholars in various disciplines, and the general public were consulted through mail; workshops on the state, regional, and national levels; and direct contact. From these contacts the standards were developed.

Social studies educators should view the standards as guides and criteria to ". . . establish integrated state, district, school, department, and classroom curriculum plans to guide instruction, learning, and assessment" (p. xvii). The intent of the standards was never meant to mandate or establish a national social studies curriculum but, rather, to provide social studies teachers a framework from which to develop appropriate instructional activities for students.

The standards are organized around ten themes separated by elementary, middle, and secondary grade levels. The following themes ensure that teachers have a conceptional design in order to create lesson and unit curricula.

   I. Culture
  II. Time, Continuity, and Change
 III. Peoples, Places, and Environments
  IV. Individual Development and Identity
   V. Individual, Groups, and Institutions
  VI. Power, Authority, and Governance
 VII. Production, Distribution, and Consumption
VIII. Science, Technology, and Society
  IX. Global Connections
   X. Civic Ideals and Practices

A list of Performance Expectations is established in each theme to help students achieve basic skill levels. We have selected two themes to serve as examples at the middle grade level: Standard II: Time, Continuity, and Change, and Standard IV: Individual Development and Identity.

In the activity "Write a Local History," students will meet the Performance Expectations in several ways. Tracing a community's history helps students locate themselves in time. By comparing historical activities to the present, students gain an understanding of how human activity changes and develops. For instance, changes in the economy of a maritime community to one of computer technology poses dramatic shifts for individuals. Student researchers begin to realize not only what happened in the past, but also how they are connected to it. Through the investigation of a local history students can compare and contrast their perspective on events with those who participated in them. All students carry a story. How do their stories reflect varying viewpoints and inform contemporary ideas and actions? This is the basis for active and responsible citizenship.

WRITE A LOCAL HISTORY

Daniel Webster once said, "It is wise to recur to the history of our ancestors. Those, who do not look upon themselves as a link connecting the past with the future, do not perform their duty to the world." Writing a local history

Write a Local History

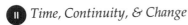 *Time, Continuity, & Change*

Social studies programs should include experiences that provide for the study of *the ways human beings view themselves in and over time*, so that the learner can:

Performance Expectations	*Related Themes*
a. Demonstrate an understanding that different scholars may describe the same event or situation in different ways but must provide reasons or evidence for their views.	I III V
b. Identify and use key concepts such as chronology, causality, change, conflict, and complexity to explain, analyze, and show connections among patterns of historical change and continuity.	I III V VIII
c. Identify and describe selected historical periods and patterns of change within and across cultures, such as the rise of civilizations, the development of transportation systems, the growth and breakdown of colonial systems, and others.	I V VIII X
d. Identify and use processes important to reconstructing and reinterpreting the past, such as using a variety of sources, providing, validating, and weighing evidence for claims, checking credibility of sources, and searching for causality.	I III X
e. Develop critical sensitivities such as empathy and skepticism regarding attitudes, values, and behaviors of people in different historical contexts.	I III V VI VII VIII IX
f. Use knowledge of facts and concepts drawn from history, along with methods of historical inquiry, to inform decision making about and action taking on public issues.	V VI VII VIII IX X

will help students view themselves as a link between the past and the future. They will show interest in activities they can see and relate to. Events that took place on a street, in a building, along a waterway, or in an adjacent field or meadow that they can visit will enable them to touch history. Historical figures can be better appreciated if students visit their houses, see the desk on which they wrote, read their manuscripts and records, and view their clothing. Every town and city has a vivid history.

Students will be able to employ four of the five themes when they research and write a local history: location, place, human–environment interaction, and movement. A detailed description of the five themes is presented in Chapter 5.

Location.   Why did Native American and early European explorers settle where they did? Living along riverbanks, in the lee of forests, near game, close to harbors—all met the basic needs for water, food, shelter, and transportation. Which of these conditions were responsible for the history of your community?

Place.   What kind of place was your community in 1600? In 1750? In 1900? Today? Students enjoy investigating old maps, looking at photographs, reading diaries and journals, and consulting local histories to aid them in writing their history. What geographical features gave rise to cultural attributes? What is the relationship between ethnic background, climate, and house type? In the same way that hogans, wickiups, adobes, and teepees reflect materials available in particular environments, the saltbox style house of New England, half-timbered house in Pennsylvania, or plantation style in the South reflect both the cultural background of the builders and the materials available. A sense of place affords middle school researchers an opportunity to investigate the rich diversity of the many cultures that came into contact when the old and new worlds collided. Every history should explore early contacts between Native Americans and early settlers and contacts between succeeding waves of immigrants. What kind of place was their community, and how did it change?

Human–Environment Interaction.   Conflicts among cultures clearly emerge when students investigate patterns of land use. The use and/or abuse of land creates many difficult questions for middle schoolers. Obviously, European expansion was inevitable, but what happens to the environment when large populations spill into new areas? How are food and shelter obtained? What are the consequences to the environment? As students wrestle with these questions, have them also consider what our relationship is to contemporary problems. Is the ecological sensitivity of earlier Native Americans helping us to solve today's problems? To what extent should citizens respect nature or continue to try to control it for societal needs? As middle schoolers delve into the expansion and development of their community, what patterns can they detect? Which of these patterns are helpful or harmful? Some communities developed in a haphazard manner; others did not. What historical forces explain these differences? As students' historical investigation blends into the present, what trends can they predict for their community in the next 25 or 30 years?

Movement.   America is a country on the move. It has a unique history of movement. How did the early settlers move to your community? Did they walk, sail on boats or barges, arrive in ox carts, ride on horseback, ride in a train, or fly on a plane? Was your community a transportation center, a jumping-off point for further expansion—or did it decline because it missed the rail line?

Movement examines tragedy and promise, from the "Trail of Tears" to the "Gold Rush." It also suggests physical movement as well as social movement. Do the rags-to-riches stories of Horatio Alger represent successful individuals in your community? Is it still possible for an ordinary person to become president? Students investigating their communities will continue to uncover the genius of inventors, politicians, and entrepreneurs that led to great wealth and power for some and tumbling fortunes for others. What events contributed to the rise and fall of local citizens? To what extent are students immune from social dislocation? Do researching and writing about local history help them with that question?

This activity will help students develop research, organization, and writing skills as they compile a local history. Two themes are presented: (1) how to select topics, and (2) how to research and write a local history.

How to Select Topics

The value of writing a local history is that the class can concentrate on areas it finds most interesting. They should not be restricted by a conventional table of contents, such as North America before the Europeans to the present.

Each town developed along different lines and at different times. Its history was as much a function of accident as it was of planning. Social, historical, and economic events influenced the development of these small communities. Let these events guide the writing of your local history.

In the process of selecting a list of topics with your class, think about the following questions and ideas. Concentrate on those that apply to your community. What events or time periods made history in your town? For many, prerevolutionary history is fascinating. The early settlers forged their way into the wilderness, endured physical hardships and defended themselves against Indian attacks during the French and Indian wars. These were the frontier settlements, and their contribution set the groundwork for a new social order.

During the colonial period, as society became prosperous, other towns and cities dominated the social and political events of the time. The larger seaboard communities with their maritime industries were influential during the American Revolution. Visits by Washington and Lafayette indicated their importance.

As the economy changed, its influence was felt. Towns and cities once famous during the American Revolution were eclipsed by burgeoning cities of the industrial revolution. The rapid demographic changes in America pushed many immigrants into industrial cities, as well as forced many out and westward to the new frontier.

Early Origins

What conditions led to the founding of a town or city, and is that influence still felt? The first settlements were located near water, either on the ocean or along rivers flowing to the sea. Fishing and lumbering were the primary industries. In many New England communities, the church was not only the ecclesiastical authority but also the civil authority. Many early towns were founded because the inhabitants did not want to walk great distances to Sunday services. Theocracies developed and remained until the early 1800s.

Other cities, such as Lowell, Lawrence, and Holyoke, Massachusetts, and Nashua and Manchester, New Hampshire, were clearly industrial cities. At the height of economic activity, the Amoskeag Mills in Manchester, New Hampshire, produced 50 miles of fabric a day. Towns along the Ohio and Mississippi Rivers were jumping-off points for westward expansion. Carl Sandburg's Chicago and Carnegie's Pittsburgh reflected the enormous economic development of the cattle and steel industries. The immigrants squeezed into the cities, their backgrounds and cultures in their baggage, giving America its distinctive regional qualities. Their contribution to local history needs to be recorded.

The expansion of the railroad, particularly after the Civil War, fueled the growth of cities. From manufacturing to distribution, the rails carried products across America. Great rail centers sprang up, and with them, a city's history. When the "golden spike" connected east with west, our culture and that of the American Indian experienced profound changes.

Economic Forces

Cities and towns rise and fall with the economy. What happened in your community during times of recession and depression? What happened when a new technology was invented? Did your town prosper or decline? How were the lives of citizens affected by economic changes? Investigate the ebb and flow of economic forces as you select your topics. Is it an appropriate area for your local history?

With these broad ideas in mind, what specific topics can be investigated in writing a local history? A cursory view of a table of contents of any local history will provide a chronology for students to follow. However, particular towns have topics peculiar to their history. The next section will represent a scattering of specific topics to consider as you continue to plan a local history.

A history of a local community is a history of the lives of a people. Knowing how they lived and what they did provides insight into the ordinary circumstances of life for most people. A study of the social history of a community reveals the reasons for its customs, habits, and mores.

Amusement and Sports

Many games and sports played in colonial America are seldom heard about today. Sports not only tell what people did in leisure time but also what values the society supported. In Lancaster, New Hampshire, two political occasions (the annual regimental muster, and the semiannual terms, in May and November, of the highest court) prompted games on a local level. People thronged the streets to watch the parade and filled the fields to participate in games. Wrestling was a big sport, inviting competition among towns. Lancaster citizens also enjoyed swimming, which included diving off the "spring board" into the flume above the saw mill, pitching "quates" (quoits), and rolling tenpins. On the Fourth of July, the townspeople made "fireballs," a domestic product made of a long candle wick and a ball of string soaked in turpentine. After dark, they would light the fireballs and quickly pass them to one another. "The rapidity of handling prevented burning hands, and deft players would soon have the air alive with fiery arcs, tangents, parabolas, and, as the balls burned out, blazing stars of fragments" (Stanley, 1987, p. 353).

Prior to urbanization, most people were dependent on the weather for survival. An early frost could ruin their harvest, storms destroyed valuable property, and lightning burned barns full of hay. In Barnstead, New Hampshire, the summer of 1769 was called the "cold summer." "Frosts were seen in every month of the year. The year after the 'cold summer,' winter came in intensely cold and remained with very deep snows for forty days in succession" (Jewett, 1872, p. 189). The year 1815 was no delight and was memorable for its deep snows. The woods were filled with 8 feet of snow, and, as late as May 19, 9 inches fell. A snowy spring was followed by a tempestuous fall. On September 23, the greatest gale ever recorded struck, blowing down much of the primeval forests. Students can imagine what effects weather had on earlier settlers and how the lives of settlers were shaped by natural forces.

Early Schools and Education

In 1647, the General Court of Massachusetts passed an act that was the basis for public education in the Bay Colony and influenced the establishment of a public school system in the other New England colonies as well. The act required that towns of 50 households or more should provide for instruction in reading and writing and went on to suggest possible ways of financing such a system. "It being one chief object of that old deluder, Satan, to keep men from the knowledge of the Scriptures" (Edwards & Richey, 1963, p. 57). From that time forward, schools and education reflected local community attitudes and values. Investigating history of schools in a local community is yet another way to understand our heritage.

"In Newfields, New Hampshire, the early schools were located in private homes, and, not infrequently, barns were used as school rooms" (Fitts, 1912, p. 328). A school in Canterbury, New Hampshire, exhibited similar problems. "Tradition has it that these school rooms were not always the best the house afforded, one being located, it is said, so near to a hog pen that the grunting of the animals frequently disturbed the teacher and pupils" (Lyford, 1912, p. 378).

Discipline has been a perennial concern. An anecdote from the *History of Pittsfield* describes an extreme situation.

> For thirty years this house stood at the corner, and then it was taken apart and moved to the eastern slope of Catamount on Berry Road, where it was settled on a ledge which provided a firm foundation for the front of the building, while the rear was supported by posts, as the ground fell rapidly toward the steep ravine but a few feet distant. A little later this precarious position proved too much of a temptation to the less academic minded pupils. One noon hour, while the teacher was away for her lunch, the boys knocked out the blocking out from under the rear of the building and before she returned they had almost succeeded in levering the whole schoolhouse into the deep ravine behind it. That did it! The teacher dismissed school and rallied the parents, who, after a short conference, decided to move the building across the road and down the hill a short distance where it was set up again, this time on a more level spot and on a firmer foundation. Here, surrounded by a stone wall on three sides, it remained, without any untoward incidents until 1862. In that year, the scholars being dissatisfied with the performance of the current teacher, one spring day pushed her outside and proceeded to wreck the interior of the building. After the damage was appraised, it was decided to discontinue school that year; nor was school held the next. (Young, 1953, p. 254)

In most of the colonies, schools were different for boys and girls. Apprentice programs for the boys and "dame" schools for the girls existed, as well as Latin schools and academies. Yet, in New Hampshire, equal opportunity was the hallmark of education. "In marked contrast with the people of other New England colonies, the settlers of New Hampshire very early made provisions for the coeducation of the sexes" (Lyford, 1912, p. 385). Lyford goes on to cite that Hampton in 1649, Dover in 1658, and Portsmouth in 1773 provided for the education of all children who were capable of learning to read, write, and cast accounts.

Students enjoy investigating how early schools were organized, run, and maintained. Let them write a section of their local history about the schools in their community, the curriculum used, types of teachers employed and their training and, of course, discipline procedures.

Accidents and Casualties

Calamities, accidents, and casualties that befell people in earlier times are other areas worthy of research. Students' imaginations are captured when they read accounts of accidents in early newspapers and local histories. Small children were frequently scalded or drowned in buckets of water. Older people were kicked by horses or run over by carriages. They fell out of trees or trees fell on them. Drownings occurred as regularly as rain, and several accounts of self-inflicted gunshot wounds pepper the pages of local histories.

In Cornish, New Hampshire, two reported accidents testify to the agricultural nature of society. "In 1858, Arthur Wyman, age thirteen, son of Milton Wyman was sliding in a field near his school house, when his sled struck a pile of frozen manure, breaking it, and a portion of it was driven into his body several inches. From the effects of this he died after a few hours of extreme suffering," and from the same account, in 1870, "8-year-old Willie Chase while playing in a barnyard was accidently hit in the head by a piece of frozen manure, which caused his death" (Child, 1910, p. 198).

Two bizarre accidents occurred involving school-age children. From a tombstone in Rye, New Hampshire, the following epitaph is inscribed, "Sheridan, Son of, Jonathan Philbrick, Esq. & Sarah, His Wife, Was Instantly Killed by Lightening, While at School, June 30, 1824, Aged 11 years." The *History of the Town of Peterborough, N.H.* reports, "On June 23, 1838, Hannah Jane, daughter of John Chapman, killed by a window sash falling upon her neck in her attempt to get into a school-house in Jaffrey. The blocking under her feet fell falling away and leaving her hung by the neck, age twelve years, five months" (p. 237).

How to Research and Write Local History

What sources should students use and why? Two basic types should be distinguished—*primary*, original documents and *secondary*, interpretive sources. Students investigating their local community can usually find primary sources at the local historical association, the public library (in the special collections section), local churches, and municipal offices. Reading original documents, records, and maps engages the students' interest and, at the same time, provides the materials used by professional historians. Students who research New England records will find an abundance of material. "For the first New Englanders, then, Puritanism and the fear of the uncivilizing ways of the wilderness account in considerable measure for the amazing proliferation of records at every level of society. This penchant for recording events in public and private life distinguishes the Colonial New Englander from his counterpart in the mid-Atlantic and southern colonies" (Crandall, 1984, p. 8). Secondary sources and interpretive histories should also be consulted to place local events into a broader social and historical context.

Sources

Newspapers.   Students should learn to read newspapers with a critical eye. The information they contain is useful, but newspapers were business enterprises, not historical journals. Profit was the primary motive. However, in spite of those concerns, newspapers do furnish valuable local information. Most libraries keep microfiche copies of local editions, as well as national editions. Copied by researchers, they can be studied at home or in the classroom.

Personal Diaries and Journals.   Historical societies and special collections sections of the public library house diaries, journals, and personal manuscripts. Some entries provide anecdotal accounts, others offer specific information, particularly if business was transacted, and a few reveal the authors' reflections of their time period. Although bias is a consideration, often these accounts are the only material available to gain an understanding of events from a personal perspective.

Records.   Municipal, state, federal, organizational, and church records provide information that help students understand local events. Tax records, street directories, vital statistics (births, deaths, and marriages), and school records are easily obtained in public libraries and municipal offices. Student interest is charged when they read documents and records in their original form.

Maps.   Villages became towns, and towns became cities. Early maps reveal the original roads, boundaries, and houses in a community. Locations of businesses, such as wharfs, grist mills, saw mills, factories, and rail depots, are identified. When students compare early maps to more recent maps of their community, demographic changes can be ascertained.

Photographs.   The camera's eye allows students to see what their community was like in previous generations. They are surprised to see the many changes that have occurred. Trees no longer stand where they once did, buildings have been replaced by shopping malls, condominium complexes have arisen in former meadows, and in some communities gentrification has replaced old neighborhoods. Focusing on business names painted on storefronts, horse-drawn wagons, hoopskirted women, laborers building by hand, and boys lazily fishing, early photographers captured for today's students a historical picture of their community. They can determine from photographs not only facts about their community but also what is missing, leading to further inquiry.

Throughout the process of researching local history, students have an obligation to strive for accuracy. The necessity of taking careful notes cannot be overemphasized. As the class data bank is filled with new information, teachers can encourage students to probe beyond just surface facts. "Explanation and interpretation add a dimension to a study that can be overlooked by the beginning historian. It is here in the interpretive analysis that students of history come face to face with the reality of their conclusions" (Stanley, 1987, pp. 340–341).

References

Child, William H. (1910). *History of the Town of Cornish*, Vol. I. Concord, NH: Rumford Press.

Cogswell, Rev. Elliot C. (1878). *History of Nottingham, Deerfield and Northwood*. Manchester, NH: John B. Clarke.

Crandall, Ralph J. (1984). *Genealogical Research in New England*. Baltimore: Genealogical Publishing Company.

Edwards, Newton, and Herman G. Richey. (1963). *The School in the American Social Order*. Boston: Houghton Mifflin.

Fitts, Rev. James Hill. (1912). *History of Newfields, N.H.* Concord, NH.

Jewett, Jeremiah P., M.D. (1872). *History of Barnstead*. Lowell, MA: Marden and Rowell, Printers.

Lyford, James Otis. (1912). *History of Canterbury, N.H., 1727–1912*. Concord, NH: The Rumford Press.

Parsons, Langdon B. (1905). *History of Rye, N.H., 1623–1903*. Concord, NH: Rumford Printing Company.

Stanley, John Clarke. (1987). "Local Schools: Exploring Their History." *History New Hampshire*, 42(4):353.

Young, Harold E. (1953). *History of Pittsfield, New Hampshire*. Concord: New Hampshire Bindery.

The second example, Theme IV: Individual Development and Identity, provides performance expectations that can be attained using the activity, "Write Your Family History."

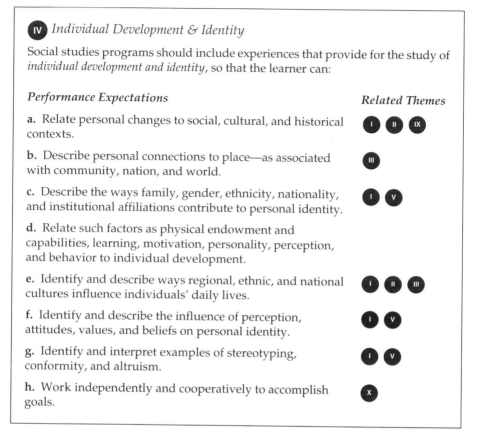

IV *Individual Development & Identity*

Social studies programs should include experiences that provide for the study of *individual development and identity*, so that the learner can:

Performance Expectations   *Related Themes*

a. Relate personal changes to social, cultural, and historical contexts.

b. Describe personal connections to place—as associated with community, nation, and world.

c. Describe the ways family, gender, ethnicity, nationality, and institutional affiliations contribute to personal identity.

d. Relate such factors as physical endowment and capabilities, learning, motivation, personality, perception, and behavior to individual development.

e. Identify and describe ways regional, ethnic, and national cultures influence individuals' daily lives.

f. Identify and describe the influence of perception, attitudes, values, and beliefs on personal identity.

g. Identify and interpret examples of stereotyping, conformity, and altruism.

h. Work independently and cooperatively to accomplish goals.

Students tracing their family's history will be able to describe personal connections to place as associated with community, nation, and world; in addition they will describe ways family, gender, ethnicity, nationality, and institutional affiliations contribute to personal identity. As one investigates further regional, ethnic, and national cultures and their influence on individuals' daily lives, a relationship can be ascertained. The questions "Who am I?" and "How do I fit into my society?" need to be answered before one can become an active and responsible citizen. "Write Your Family History" attempts to move students in that direction.

WRITE YOUR FAMILY HISTORY

Where did your family come from? From the Mayflower or from an overcrowded ocean liner in 1910? Are they Italian, Irish, or Old Yankee? Why did they come to America? Every family has a history and a story. This genealogical activity presents the student with an immediate problem, but because of its generative nature, it can provide students with a lifetime of research and pleasure. In the process of writing a family history, students will become interested in aspects of history, economics, geography, and psychology that affected the lives of their ancestors. More important, students begin to understand their relationship to history.

All five themes can be employed in helping students investigate their own family. Ask students to locate precisely where particular family members lived and when. Use push pins on a world map to show where family members live today. Once students have located the origin of their family ask them to describe what kind of place it was. This task involves research. Answer the following questions:

1. What was the environment like?
2. What economic conditions led to emigration?
3. Were family members persecuted for social, political, or religious reasons?

Our students reflect a multicultural society. This activity will provide the base for better understanding what students have in common and reasons for understanding differences.

Once students can describe the place in which their ancestors lived, they are ready to investigate the reasons for their leaving. Push-pull factors drive people across countries and over continents. Student research will reveal the reasons why their ancestors left their homeland. What risks did family members take in the hope of bettering their condition? Every subculture in America has its unique set of circumstances, and every student is a product of that cultural heritage. A well-researched family history helps students find the connection to their past.

New cultures flooded in successive waves onto the American continent. As the population pressed westward, spilling into every corner of our country, Native Americans were displaced, rivers polluted, timber cut, and agricultural land exhausted. In short, the once pristine character of our country was severely altered. What impact did immigration have on our land as an industrial society was created? What problems exist today? And how should they be solved? People–environment interaction is a powerful theme to use in this activity. It provides students and teachers with immeasurable learning possibilities.

We the People: An Atlas of America's Ethnic Diversity (Allen & Turner, 1988) illustrates the fact that America is composed of ethnic regions. Although boundaries are not clear-cut, students will find that specific ethnic populations settled in particular areas of the country. The largest concentrations of Native Americans live in the Southwest and in the northern tier states of

Oregon, Montana, North and South Dakota, Minnesota, Wisconsin, and New York State. Students of French ancestry will probably live in Northern New England or Louisiana, whereas German and Scandanavian descendents most likely live in the upper Midwest.

The West Coast reflects ethnic diversity more than any other region in the country. Spanish influence dominated early in California's history. More recently, Chinese, Japanese, and Southeast Asians have emigrated to the West Coast. What factors were responsible for the regional pattern of immigration?

Teachers can seize the opportunity to encourage students to conduct further research or teach lessons that show the relationship between a student's ancestors and larger regional or national events. Swept in a wave of history, ancestors were subjected to many forces. Several examples will serve to illustrate.

1. Is your last name Irish? Quite possibly, your family came to America during the 1840 Potato Famine in Ireland. Understanding the economic forces that contributed to a major migration, the impact the Irish have on America, and how they were initially received, are bits of the cloth of America's fabric.
2. Perhaps your family is Franco-American, lived and worked in the New England mills after immigrating from Canada. What events caused them to move? How did they maintain their cultural and religious heritage after arriving?
3. If you are Black and live in the North, did your family migrate from the South, or are they original descendents of the first Black slaves in the North? Did they leave the South after the Civil War, or were they some of the few who used the Underground Railroad?
4. In one author's case, his great-grandmother had a piece of silk from the Orient that she had received from her great-grandfather, who was a ship's captain. Her mothers' maiden name was Mary Anna Townsend. In the process of attempting to determine if the author is related to the famous War of 1812 privateer, Penn Townsend, he has learned a lot about local history as well as national events.

Writing a family history poses many questions for further investigations. Why did the family move? Why doesn't that town exist anymore? What effect did wars, economic conditions, family struggles, deaths, and so on have on family members? In what ways were their lives changed because of these events? Once the pot begins to boil, it will continue to do so throughout a lifetime.

This activity is divided into five topic areas. Mastering these areas will enable a student to conduct a family investigation along the lines of a professional genealogist, as follows:

1. Pedigree chart
2. Family history
3. Research
4. Problems
5. Interdisciplinary activities

Pedigree Chart

A pedigree chart is a visual representation of one's family. Similar to a map, it provides structure and direction. A student can easily see the relationship between a great-grandmother on the maternal side and an uncle on the paternal side. In this way, blood lines are traced and understood. Two types of pedigree charts are the common ancestor chart and the present generation chart.

The present generation chart is best for students to use. It begins with the student. The present-generation pedigree chart is used as a formal instrument when the activity is complete. The "working chart" is just that. During the stages of inquiry it is used for notes, comments, or leads. The present-generation pedigree chart is presented first.

			Great-Grandfather
		Grandfather	
			Great-Grandmother
	Father		
			Great-Grandfather
		Grandmother	
			Great-Grandmother
You			
			Great-Grandfather
		Grandfather	
			Great-Grandmother
	Mother		
			Great-Grandfather
		Grandmother	
			Great-Grandmother

Research begins at home. Students fill in the chart. They list when and where family members were born, married, and died. When the chart is as complete as possible, the next phase begins, collecting data on family members and the institutions to which they belonged. For this activity, students will want to use a working chart. The chart allows students space to record family names and vital dates. In conjunction with the chart, students should keep an organized notebook or cards to record pertinent information.

                        Grandfather
                        born
                        worked
                        married
        Father   died

                        Grandmother
                        born
                        worked
                        married
                        died
    You
                        Grandfather
                        born
                        worked
                        married
                        died

        Mother
                        Grandmother
                        born
                        worked
                        married
                        died

Family History

The family is often the best source for gathering information. Usually someone has kept family records, collected newspaper clippings or scrapbooks, or retained possession of the old family Bible. Seek that person out. As the web is spun, it will eventually encompass older, distant relatives. Third cousin Margaret may have photographs of a family reunion taken in 1925, or a hastily penned note concerning her Aunt Nett's bout with yellow fever. Family tradition is a good source for the beginning student researcher. Information gathered from the present generation is easy to obtain and confirm. However, as one steps back into the lives of earlier ancestors, the anecdotes are less reliable and more difficult to corroborate. Once a relative has told a version of an event or recounted a story told to him or her, it is time to check the information. No matter how believable some stories seem, they may contain inaccuracies. Gilbert Doane (1960), in his book, *Searching for Your Ancestors*, relates a story written by an aged grandmother on the history of her family:

> Here is all Grandma can think of about the forefathers. Lord John Whiting, Great Grandfather, was born in 1735, near London. He came to America on the May Flower in 1776 soon after the Revolutionary War, bringing his two daughters Lady Jane and Mabel (Not sure of the name). She, Mabel, went back to England with her father.
>
> Lord Whiting bought some land in Connecticut and gave it to Lady Jane for a wedding present when she married Grandfather James Dupey. He was a French nobleman in 1796 or 1798. James Dupey was Captain of the May Flower. Ten sons were born to them. (pp. 30–31)

Ask the following questions to verify information. Are the dates correct? Do other sources state similar claims? Some of this information will create amusement as well as information, as does this one: "John the son of John Warner and of Mahittabel his wife was borne December ye:18th:1716; Daniell ye sone of John Warnor and of Mahittabel his wife was born May ye:6th:1717" (Doane, 1960, p. 8). After conversations with relatives have been exhausted, start searching through family records. Family histories, bulletins of organizations, and family Bibles contain information that is usually accurate. The family Bible recorded the important events in one's life and often had notes scribbled in the margins. Based on Jones, Eakle, and Christensen (1972), the following survey suggests an infinite number of family sources that can be used to obtain information on relatives.

Research

By now students have amassed a lot of information using the pedigree chart and family records. Of course, there are gaps. Blood lines might appear to terminate, because no one could recall a great-grandfather's mother's maiden name. Determine what to do next. Do students want to follow their mother's family or perhaps spend time researching one generation in the 1840s? Define the research objective.

Family research is complex and exceedingly time-consuming. Middle schoolers should select one *manageable* aspect of their family that intrigues them and bear in mind the following guidelines:

1. Select a family problem.
2. List sources that are accessible.
3. Determine a realistic time for completion.

Survey Outline

Pedigree Ancestors   *Birth Data and Place*

_____

_____

_____

HOME JURISDICTION: (Immediate, Family, Friends, Close Relatives, Associates)

Those I Can Personally Visit   *Those I Must Correspond With*

HOME SOURCES:
This checklist is a guide to the records you should find in the homes of your relatives. Check (√) each record you search. Write additional sources you may discover in the empty blanks.

Personal Records	*Legal Papers*	*Certificates*
_____ Journal	_____ Will	_____ Birth
_____ Diary	_____ Deeds	_____ Marriage
_____ Biography	_____ Land Grants	_____ Death
_____ Patriarchal Blessing	_____ Water Rights	_____ Divorce
_____ Letters	_____ Mortgages	_____ Adoption
_____ Seal	_____ Leases	_____ Graduation
_____ Photographs	_____ Bonds	_____ Christening
_____ Autograph Album	_____ Loans	_____ Blessing
_____ Personal Knowledge	_____ Contracts	_____ Baptism
_____ Baby Book	_____ Summons	_____ Confirmation
_____ Wedding Book	_____ Subpoena	_____ Ordination
_____ Scrapbooks	_____ Tax Notices	_____ Transfer
_____ Funeral Book	_____ Guardian Papers	_____ Ministerial
_____ Guest Register	_____ Abstracts of Title	_____ Mission Release
_____ Travel Account	_____	_____ Membership
_____ Treasures of Truth	_____	_____ Apprenticeship
_____ Book Plates	_____	_____ Achievement
_____		_____ Award
_____		_____

Survey Outline   *Continued*

Military Records
_____ Service
_____ Pension
_____ Disability
_____ Discharge
_____ National Guard
_____ Selective Service
_____ Bounty Award
_____ Service Medals
_____ Ribbons
_____ Sword
_____ Firearms
_____ Uniforms
_____ Citations
_____ Separation Papers
_____

Citizenship Papers
_____ Naturalization
_____ Denization
_____ Alien Registration
_____ Deportment
_____ Passport
_____ Visa
_____ Vaccination
_____

School Records
_____ Diplomas
_____ Report Cards
_____ Honor Roll
_____ Awards
_____ Transcripts
_____ Yearbooks
_____ Publications
_____

Employment Records
_____ Apprenticeship
_____ Awards
_____ Graduation
_____ Citations
_____ Severance Papers
_____ Social Security
_____ Retirement Papers
_____ Pension
_____ Union
_____ Income Tax
_____

Family Records
_____ Bible
_____ Books of Remembrance
_____ Family Group Sheets
_____ Pedigrees
_____ Genealogies
_____ Temple Record Books
_____ Family Bulletins
_____ Family Histories
_____ Printed Histories
_____ MS Histories
_____ Local Histories
_____ Family Traditions
_____ "Birth Briefs"
_____

Announcements
_____ Wedding
_____ Birth
_____ Death
_____ Funeral
_____ Graduation
_____ Divorce
_____ Anniversary
_____ Memorial Cards
_____ New Job
_____ Travel
_____ New Home
_____ Birthday
_____ Professional
_____ Engagement
_____

Newspaper Clippings
_____ Announcements
_____ Obituaries
_____ Special Events
_____ Vital Statistics
_____ Home Town Papers
_____ Professional
_____ Trade
_____

Membership Records
_____ Cards
_____ Publications
_____ Programs
_____ Uniforms
_____ Awards
_____ Certificates
_____

Financial Records
_____ Accounts
_____ Bills
_____ Receipts
_____ Check Stubs
_____ Estate Records
_____

Health Records
_____ X-rays
_____ Insurance Papers
_____ Hospital Records
_____ Medical Records
_____ Immunizations
_____

Licenses
_____ Business
_____ Occupation
_____ Professional
_____ Hunting
_____ Firearms
_____ Driver's
_____ Motor Vehicle
_____

Household Items
_____ Silverware
_____ Needlework
_____ Sampler
_____ Tapestries
_____ Dishes
_____ Friendship Quilt
_____ Coat of Arms
_____ Insignias
_____ Souvenirs
_____ Clothing
_____ Tools
_____ Memorial Rings
_____ Engraved Jewelry
_____

Books
_____ Atlases
_____ Yearbooks
_____ Textbooks
_____ Prizes
_____ Treasured Volumes
_____ Vocational
_____ Foreign Language
_____

Copyright 1972 Genealogical Copy Service.

An actual investigation serves as an example. Family tradition has it that at the age of 11, Great-Great Uncle Page Sumner sat in an apple tree and watched the Confederate Army advance through the Manoghesey Valley and engage in battle with Union troops. The problem: Did Uncle Page Sumner actually witness the battle? To determine if he did, examine the following:

What Sources Are Accessible?
1. Interview the family members who told the story. Do dates and time check with history?
2. To determine if Uncle Page was 11 years old during the Civil War and lived in that part of the country, check family history, letters, births, deaths, church records, and census data.
3. Look at Civil War records and newspaper accounts.
4. Write a narrative describing the family member and the event he observed, assuming other sources confirm the story.

What Is the Time Frame?
1. Plan time for local research.
2. Plan time to send and receive letters from distant family members.
3. Is the family traveling to visit relatives or the city or town in which events unfolded?

Problems

Genealogical research is fraught with problems. Do not believe everything you read until it has been corroborated, and be particularly skeptical of anecdotes that have filtered down through family history. Most would rather believe that an ancestor was a famous patriot instead of a common crook. Many families are blessed with both. Family skeletons need to be exhumed from closets to keep company with their more honored relatives if accuracy and understanding are to be achieved.

Family tradition is the first problem. Although there is an element of truth in many stories that are handed down, the actual circumstances, when held to close scrutiny, are quite different from the tale told. In *Pitfalls in Genealogical Research*, Milton Rubicam (1987) illustrates the problem:

> Many English and American families named Hall have traditionally claimed descent from William Shakespeare through his elder daughter Susanna, wife of Dr. John Hall. The fact remains, however, that the Bard of Stratford-on-Avon does not have a single descendant living today. The last member of his direct line was his granddaughter,

Elizabeth Hall, wife of Sir John Barnard (Bernard) who was buried on 17 February 1669/70. (p. 16)

Students must be wary when using family tradition as a single source.

Another problem that is vexing for the researcher is the confusion that surrounds people with the same name, living in the same place, and being of approximately the same age. Rubicam (1987) cites an interesting example:

In his article "Too Many Jonathan Gilletts in Windsor Connecticut," *TAG*, 56:72–79 (April, 1980), he listed seventeen men by the name of Jonathan Gillett who lived in Windsor from before 1677–1777. These include four pairs of brothers who never met each other, the elder of each pair having died before the birth of the younger. (p. 34)

In a less complicated example, my own research has located several Townsends who are listed as ship's captains and mariners; who had wives named May Anna, Mary Ann, or Marianna; and who lived within three blocks of one another. Time and patience are required to unravel these initial confusions.

In addition to confusion over names and persons, words and their meanings also change over time. Rubicam (1987) has devoted an entire chapter to this issue (pp. 37–42). A few examples, taken from this chapter, are necessary to appreciate the problem. *Mr.* and *Mrs.* were originally reserved for persons of social position. *Master* or *Mister* are the correct attributions and were strictly applied to the landed gentry, members of the clergy, and public officials. *Mrs.* (Mistress) was applied to both married and unmarried women. In the eighteenth century, *spinster* was used to designate both wife and widow. Today it has two meanings: a woman who spins thread, and an unmarried woman.

Name changes are very elusive. A list of sixty-seven names of occupations is provided in *The Source: A Guidebook to American Genealogy* (Eakle & Cerny, 1986, p. 342). Among them are *Ale-draper* (Inn keeper), *Backster/Baxter* (female baker), *Barker* (tanner of shoes), *Flescher* (butcher), *Hind* (farm laborer; household or domestic servant), and *Wright* (a constructor, such as a shipwright). Language changes, such as the ones listed, do arise unexpectedly, but for the neophyte researcher they create interest and information.

Interdisciplinary Activities

The family is a subject that can be explored in literature and writing. "Family literature, then, is a piece of writing—prose, poetry, or drama—that emphasizes the family and sees the individual as part of a larger family unit whether over one or several generations" (Gouldrup, 1987, p. 1). Getting to understand families better can be accomplished several ways. The first is through student work. A journal or diary, its pages brown and brittle like autumn's leaves, set the scene for a short story. Imaginative writers create conflict and resolution, and a story is born. Ink-stained, splotchy, old letters, Rorschach-like, evoke images that lift the words from the page into poetry. Give students opportunities to let their imaginations wander through the past.

In the second way, students will want to read good literature, poetry, and drama after having struggled with their pieces. Gouldrup (1987) provides an excellent bibliography in his book, *Writing the Family Narrative*, for this purpose. A poem by Edith Mendez entitled "Tenement Mother" is an example of the power that is achieved through poetry.

Tenement Mother[1]
Hands chafed by ribbed washboard
she labored late over iron tub
until back and legs gave.
Nights she walked rough wooden floors
tending her brood. Sweet tea
for small complaints, cool hands
for fevered head.
Her heart wore down bearing children
two years apart; one held in arms,
a second tugging at her skirt,
the third kicking in her womb.
Cautioned she would not survive
another birth, her husband said
nature will not be denied.
In her fortieth year she bore
her eighth. Heart broken, she died. (p. 69)

References

Allen, James, and Eugene James Turner. (1988). *We the People: An Atlas of America's Ethnic Diversity*. New York: Macmillan.

Doane, Gilbert. (1960). *Searching for Your Ancestors*. Minneapolis: University of Minnesota Press.

Eakle, Arlene, and John Cerny, eds. (1986). *The Source: A Guidebook to American Genealogy*. Salt Lake City, UT: Ancestry Publishing.

Gouldrup, Lawrence P. (1987). *Writing the Family Narrative*. Salt Lake City, UT: Ancestry Publishing.

---

[1]Reprinted from Lawrence P. Gouldrup (1987), *Writing the Family Narrative*. Salt Lake City, UT: Ancestry Publishing, with permission courtesy of Ancestry Incorporated.

Jones, Vincent L., Arlene H. Eakle, and Mildred H. Christensen. (1972). *Family History for Fun and Profit*. Provo, UT: Community Press.
Rubicam, Milton. (1987). *Pitfalls in Genealogical Research*. Salt Lake City, UT: Ancestry Publishing.

NATIONAL GEOGRAPHY STANDARDS

The third example, "People and Their Environment: Searching the Historical Record," addresses two geographic standards. *National Geography Standards: Geography for Life* (1994) was developed after a decade of reform in geographic education. "There is widespread acceptance among people of the United States that being literate in geography is essential if students are to leave schools equipped to earn a decent living, enjoy the richness of life, and participate responsibly in local, national, and international affairs" (*Geography for Life*, p. 9). Eighteen standards were developed for middle-level students (*Geography for Life*, pp. 143–182). Standard 14: How Human Actions Modify the Physical Environment and Standard 15: How Physical Systems Affect Human Systems are used to illustrate how students might begin to understand the plight of the Anasazi on Mesa Verde.

People and Their Environment: Searching the Historical Record

What precipitated the demise of the ancient Anasazi culture after nearly 800 years of their successful cultural adaptation to the harsh environment of our desert Southwest? From recent archeological evidence, researchers suggest that a combination of factors led to the migration of the "Ancient Ones" from the Mesa Verde. The story of the Anasazi began around A.D. 500 and ended rather abruptly in A.D. 1300 with their abandonment of the cliff dwellings they had so painfully and carefully constructed barely 100 years earlier. After a cursory review of the historical record, we realized that the experience of the Anasazis was not unique to their culture group and that we could learn from their long-ago decisions (Allen, 1997; Allen & Stevens, 1996).

When we endeavor to promote in our students a commitment to active and responsible citizenship by developing their keen awareness of the profound relationship between humans and their physical environment (e.g., *CAAP in Action: The Environment*, 1991), the story of the Anasazi may serve as an example of the possible consequences of human activity on the physical environment. One example of the impact of human activity on the earth may be instructive for our students to help them develop their understanding of this critical reality. The Anasazi story holds lessons for all of us and can excite our students' imaginations. For a study of the Anasazi people, we have devised some concrete questions and examples of projects to spur students to absorb the information about these early inhabitants and apply the implications of their experiences to modern life.

The People and Their Environment: A Case Study

The Anasazi on Mesa Verde.   The rich archeological legacy left behind by the Anasazi remains mute testimony to both the positive and negative impact of human activity on the physical environment. Cultural adaptation is an essential tool for human survival, although from time to time even a refined and timely response to environmental changes is insufficient to preserve human habitation in a specific region of the earth. The development and subsequent abandonment of the cliff dwellings at Mesa Verde by the Anasazi around A.D. 1300 is a case in point.

The Anasazi way of life and their interaction with their environment may be traced through a series of developments. During their hunter-gatherer stage, the Anasazi were at one with their environment. Essentially nomadic, the family groups migrated from place to place in a loose confederation, searching for plant and animal foods to nourish and sustain themselves. Life was precarious at best, a kind of hand-to-mouth existence. When food sources played out because of excessive consumption, drought, or increased population, the family groups moved to another area in the region (Wenger, 1980).

Following a series of cultural adaptations, such as the use of clay pottery to store wild grains, the replacement of the atlatl with bows and arrows, and the rudimentary cultivation of food crops, the Anasazis' hunter-gatherer patterns slowly evolved to a more sedentary way of life. The introduction of cultivated crops, such as beans, corn, and squash, and trade with the other native tribes to the south in present-day Mexico resulted in their slow shift to a more agriculturally based lifestyle. That transition fundamentally altered their relationship to the land that so long had sustained them. With their more settled lifestyle came the need for more permanent housing for the slowly increasing population. Although the change was not immediately evident, these cultural adaptations gradually changed the relationship between the Anasazi and their land. The ultimate impact of disturbing the delicate balance between the use and abuse of the land took several hundred years to manifest itself fully.

Cultural Development: From Caves to Cliff Dwellings

From the point at which their nomadic lifestyle began to change, the Anasazi culture may be traced through four developmental periods (Breternitz and Smith 1975, p. 56). The first stage, the Basketmakers (1–450 A.D.), evolved with their planting of corn and squash in small fields cut out of the mesa tops.

Because corn, when dried, could be stored over winter, a less nomadic existence became possible for the Anasazi. Hand-woven baskets became their all-purpose tools for carrying and storing foodstuffs; hence, the name of this cultural period for the Anasazi. The baskets enabled the Anasazi to store cultivated and harvested crops and foraged grains and other wild plant products for long periods of time.

The atlatl was the Anasazi's principal weapon for killing wild animals, the major source of protein in their diet. This weapon consisted of a long, single shaft of wood with a rawhide sling on one end in which the hunter placed a stone projectile. The hunter then used the atlatl like a spear or javelin, launching the stone projectile in a throwing motion in an effort to kill his prey. Although this weapon had a limited range of effectiveness, especially when compared to the bow and arrow, the Anasazi used it successfully in killing wild game. Meager crops of corn and squash were supplemented by foraging for wild plant foods such as berries and roots. During this period, caves, rock depressions, and sandstone overhangs along canyon walls served as places of shelter for the Anasazi.

During the second developmental period, called the Modified Basketmaker Period (450–750 A.D.), the Anasazi moved from the caves and sandstone overhangs to pithouses. They made and used pottery (clay-based vessels) and adopted the bow and arrow as a hunting tool. As they discovered the fertility of soil on the mesa tops, they began to plant more and more of their crops there. The logical transition was for them to begin living on the same mesa tops because it was easier to care for their cultivated crops.

Pithouses, consisting of a pit laborously dug with a stick and by hand in the heavy clay soil and roofed over by a mixture of clay and wood, were constructed on the Mesa Verde, which were relatively flat. Entry was by a small opening on one side of the pit, and smoke from fires in the central firepit escaped from the pithouse through a small opening in the crude roof. The structure provided much more protection from the heat and sun of summer and the cold and snow of winter than caves or rock overhangs that the Anasazi had previously used for shelter. The remnants of a number of these original pithouses exist today in Mesa Verde National Park.

The use of pottery vessels for holding and storing food and water and for cooking affected the Anasazi way of life by enabling them to store food and water for much longer periods of time than had previously been possible when they used woven baskets. Their learning how to use the bow and arrow as a tool for killing wild game enabled the Anasazi to procure their food supply at a greater distance from the Mesa Verde. Such technological advances resulted in increased population of Anasazi who were further sustained by increased food availability and better housing conditions. In short, such technological advances enabled the environment to sustain the larger number of inhabitants.

By the third developmental period, the Developmental Pueblo Period (750–1100 A.D.), large clan groups were living in long, interconnected pueblos on the mesa tops. During this time period, the Anasazi altered their housing structures from living "in" the earth (pithouses) to living "on" the earth (interconnected pueblos). Fields of crops were planted over the tops of mesas. Beans were added to corn and squash as an important part of the Anasazi diet. These crops were watered not only by the natural rainfall that averaged nineteen inches a year but also be ingenious forms of irrigation canals and reservoirs.

The shift from the Basketmaker and Modified Basketmaker patterns of life to the Pueblo (Spanish for *village*) reflects the Anasazi's transition to full village life, complete with extended family groups and clans. These changes were the result of more and varied foodstuffs in the diet, vessels for the long-term storage of these foodstuffs, more efficient weapons, and more protective housing structures.

The final developmental period of the Anasazi culture, the Great Pueblo Period (1100–1300 A.D.), proved to be their last. During the early decades of this period, the Anasazi engaged in extensive cultivation of beans, corn, and squash, cultivating every available bit of arable land and continuing to extend irrigation canals from the various water-holding pits so laborously dug into the mesa top to collect and store rainfall and storm runoff. The delicate balance between the Anasazi and their environment began to shift as the population increased further and the changing climate patterns (recurring droughts) resulted in substantial shortfalls in crop production. Drought conditions and overhunting also reduced the numbers of wild game.

This was the period of the great cliff dwellings found in today's Mesa Verde National Park in the Four Corners region of Southwestern United States (Smith, 1988). Archeological evidence strongly suggests that the Anasazi moved off the mesa tops in order to free up land for crop cultivating during that time of population increase and drought, both of which placed great pressure on them to produce more food to feed more people.

The semiarid region of the desert Southwest has, in recorded history at least, always been marginal land for human habitation. Because of an annual rainfall of less than nineteen inches, those living off the land by hunting and gathering or by the cultivation of agricultural crops had a very slim margin for error. As the Anasazi settled down on the land, their numbers increased, thus setting off a vicious cycle requiring greater and greater food resources and more water.

Through the science of dendrochronology, which is the study of tree ring evidence to ascertain old weather and climate patterns, scientists have determined that during the latter stages of the Great Pueblo Period, the desert Southwest experienced a series of extended droughts (Breternitz and Smith 1975, pp. 75–76). The impact of drought on the Anasazi way of life was devastating to their crop production and the availability of wild animals and plants for human consumption. The Anasazi soon ran short of the food that is necessary to feed a large population.

Archaeological evidence suggests that, in the absence of any identifiable enemies, the Anasazi moved out of their cliff dwellings for two reasons. First, the changing daily weather and climate patterns resulted in long-term drought conditions in the region. Second, the impact on the population of the dwindling crop harvests caused by the weather and climate changes necessitated a shift in location. By moving down into the cliff areas, the Anasazi were able to remain in the same general area for a while longer because they freed up more land for planting, which temporarily reduced the "people pressure" on the mesa environment. At the end of the thirteenth century, however, the Anasazi were forced to abandon their majestic cliff dwellings, migrating in different-sized groups south into present-day Arizona, New Mexico, and, possibly, Mexico.

The Anasazi were challenged by population increases and various technological advances to balance the delicate relationship between human needs and available environmental resources. Mostafa K. Tolba, executive director of the United Nations Programme, has succinctly stated the problem: "Land degradation is a key problem, most often caused by excessive pressure on fragile ecosystems taking too much from the land and putting back too little. But people often have too little choice. As populations grow [thereby] increasing demand for food and other essential crops, subsistence farmers in many countries are forced to overexploit their land just to survive" (Crews and Cancellier, 1991, p. 40).

The problem was further complicated by the foreboding reality of desertification. Drought and an overworked ecosystem have always contributed to a dramatic decrease in the biological potential of our planet's regions. An overworked ecosystem is created in three ways: "the use of wood as fuel, the clearing of land for farming purposes, and overgrazing" (Crews and Cancellier, 1991, p. 28). When they attempted to solve their problems at the end of the thirteenth century, the archeological records strongly suggest that the Anasazi had few viable options.

Challenging Students' Thinking

Students in social studies at all school levels may profitably explore the relationship between the Anasazi and their physical environment. If students search the historical record for concrete examples of ecologically based human dislocation, they can accomplish a number of important educational tasks. Such a search would provide students with an essential information base from which they can view not only the past but also the present. It would offer students the opportunity to appreciate the "repeating" nature of life in the relationship between people and their environment. Students would have an opportunity to refine their research, critical thinking, and extrapolation skills. Such a study would also challenge students to become involved in some meaningful way with issues facing many peoples today. The study could be an opportunity to study carefully one of the most critical influences on the quality of life and of human existence.

After a review of this case study, students should endeavor to understand how and why people make such life-threatening choices. From the case study, the students may gain some insight into our own situation, especially in the global context in which we live. Population pressure, the dwindling gap between the number of people and the food needed to feed them, loss of arable land and topsoil, and changing weather/climate patterns and their resultant impact on day-to-day life demand a rational response. Understanding the Anasazi experience can help us frame a reasoned response to problems that now affect all of us.

A good beginning is simply to learn about these peoples' experiences because they are so instructive. We can begin by asking questions, and we can review the historical experiences described in the case study in relation to the recently announced geography standards.

The National Geography Standards

In the *National Geography Standards* (1994), we find a framework for helping students to understand the impact of geography on the daily lives of people and cultures. Some suggestions for activities related to certain sample standards follow.

Standard 14: How Human Actions Modify the Physical Environment. Analyze the environmental consequences of humans changing the physical environment. List and describe the environmental effects of the Anasazi on the following physical systems: the biosphere (e.g., effects of deforestation and reduction in biodiversity); the lithosphere (e.g., effects of land degradation); the hydrosphere (e.g., groundwater decline). Evaluate the ways in which technology influences human capacity to modify the physical environment.

Analyze the environmental consequences of the intended and unintended outcomes of the major technological developments found in the Anasazi culture from 1 A.D. to 1300 A.D., such as hunting tools (e.g., the atlatl was replaced by the bow and arrow); food and water storage (e.g., woven baskets were replaced by clay pottery); housing structures (e.g., from cave to pithouse to pueblo to cliff dwelling).

Standard 15: How Physical Systems Affect Human Systems. Analyze ways in which the Anasazi developed new systems in response to conditions in their environment. Collect visual and data patterns of the land use, the economic livelihood, and the architectural styles of the Anasazi and similar information from the students' community to determine how such patterns reflect the impact of the physical environment on human systems.

Compare the Anasazi's agricultural production system (crop irrigation in a semiarid environment) with the different agricultural systems in use today (slash and burn in tropical rainforests; truck farming in the United States; and grain production in Argentina, Canada, and Ukraine).

Speculate on the effects of an undesirable change in the physical environment (e.g., extended drought) on the Anasazi and suggest how they might have mitigated the problem.

Related Questions

1. Did the Anasazi recognize a good place to live when they found it? Ask the students to analyze the choices made by the Anasazi as they adapted to the demands of an agriculturally based way of life and the technological development of stone tools, the bow and arrow, woven baskets, and clay pottery. Students need to understand that there was a complex web of interrelated decisions and events over which the Anasazi attempted unsuccessfully to exert influence. For example, expanded irrigation projects widened the gap between prosperity and starvation, as did various technological advances related to food storage (e.g., the shift from woven baskets to clay pottery enabled the Anasazi to store larger quantities of food for a longer period of time, thus providing a "food cushion" on which to rely in times of drought). In the end, their attempts at change proved futile.

Closing Thoughts

In this example, we have provided a basic outline of the interaction between the Anasazi and their environment. Other sources of information about the people of the Mesa Verde are listed below. We must ask ourselves and our students if we are doomed to repeat the life-changing situations found in the story of the Anasazi and if we have learned from their experience. Before we can challenge people to change their attitudes about the environment, we must lead them to an understanding of the impact of human habitation on that environment. By providing our students with opportunities to view the problems related to our impact on the physical environment and to seek appropriate solutions, we can stimulate their higher-order thinking, deepen their understanding of this complex reality, and help them make the connections between the past and the present.

Resources for Teaching About the Anasazi

Ambler, J. R. (1977). *The Anasazi, Prehistoric People of the Four Corners Region.* Flagstaff, AZ: Museum of Northern Arizona.

Ferguson, W. M., and A. H. Rohn. (n.d.). *Anasazi Ruins of the Southwest in Color*. Albuquerque: University of New Mexico Press.

Fletcher, M. S. (ed.). (1977). *The Wetherills of the Mesa Verde: Autobiography of Benjamin Alfred Wetherill*. Lincoln: University of Nebraska Press.

Geographic Education National Implementation Project. (1989). *7–12 Geography: Themes, Key Ideas, and Learning Opportunities*. Skokie, IL: Rand McNally Educational Publishing Division.

Jackson, C. S. (1947). *Picture Maker of the Old West: William Jackson*. New York: Charles Scribner's Sons.

Lister, R. H. (1968). Archeology for the Layman and Scientists at Mesa Verde. *Science, 160*, No. 382.

Lister, R. H., and F. C. Lister. (1983). *Those Who Came Before*. Tucson: University of Arizona Press.

McNitt, F. (1966). *Richard Wetherill Anasazi*, 2nd ed. Albuquerque: University of New Mexico Press.

Nordenskiold, G. (1893). (Reprint 1979). *The Cliff Dwellers of the Mesa Verde*. Glorietta, NM: Rio Grande Press.

Ortiz, A. (ed.). (1979). *Handbook of North American Indians (Southwest)*, Vol. 9. Washington, DC: Smithsonian Institution.

Our National Parks: Mesa Verde. (1985). Pleasantville, NY: Reader's Digest Association.

Roberts, D. (1993). "Reverse Archaeologists are Tracing the Footsteps of a Cowboy-Explorer." National Parks Division of World Wide Research & Publishing Co. *Smithsonian*, December, pp. 28–39.

Schneider, D. M., ed. 1966. *An Introduction to American Archeology: Vol. I. North and Middle America*. Englewood Cliffs, NJ: Prentice-Hall.

Smith, D. A. (1988). *Mesa Verde National Park: Shadows of the Centuries*. Lawrence: University of Kansas.

Tamarin, A., and S. Glubok. (1975). *Ancient Indians of the Southwest*. New York: Doubleday.

Watson, D. (1955). *Indians of the Mesa Verde*. Mesa Verde National Park, CO: Mesa Verde Museum Association.

Wenger, G. (1980). *The Story of Mesa Verde National Park*. Mesa Verde National Park, CO: Mesa Verde Museum Association.

Wenger, S. R. (1976). *Flowers of Mesa Verde National Park*. Mesa Verde National Park, CO: Mesa Verde Museum Association.

References

Allen, M. (1997). "The Anasazi at Mesa Verde: Life on the Green Table Then and Now." Unpublished manuscript.

Allen, M., and R. Stevens. (1996). "People and Their Environment: Searching the Historical Record." *The Social Studies, 87*(4): 156–160.

Breternitz, D. A., and J. E. Smith. (1975). "Mesa Verde: The Green Table." In *National Parkways: Mesa Verde and Rocky Mountain*. Casper, WY: National Parks, Division of World Wide Research and Publishing.

CAAP in Action: The Environment. (1991). Alexandria, VA: Close-Up Foundation.

Crews, K., and P. Cancellier, eds. (1991). *Connections: Linking Population and the Environment*. Washington, DC: Population Reference Bureau.

National Geography Standards: Geography for Life. 1994. Geography Education Standards Project. American Geographical Society, Association of American Geographers, National Council for Geographic Education and National Geographic Society, pp. 171–175; 179–180.

Smith, D. 1988. *Mesa Verde National Park: Shadow of the Centuries*. Lawrence: University Press of Kansas.

Wenger, G. 1980. *The Story of Mesa Verde National Park*. Mesa Verde National Park, CO: Mesa Verde Museum Association.

COMMUNITY INVOLVEMENT

Early adolescence is a developmental period flush with opportunities for promoting democratic attitudes and values consistent with active and responsible citizenship through a carefully designed and organized social studies program. The unifying motifs of any middle school social studies program ought to recognize the following early adolescence characteristics: (1) concern with self—development of self-esteem and a strong sense of identity; (2) concern for right and wrong—development of ethics; (3) concern for others—development of group and other-centeredness; and (4) concern for the world—development of a global perspective ("Social Studies in the Middle School," 1991).

From among numerous examples of extant social studies scope and sequence plans ("Designing a Social Studies Scope and Sequence for the 21st Century," 1986; National Council for the Social Studies, 1990), one may conclude that the stated goals of social studies instruction may be achieved through a variety of curricula and instructional methodologies.

Examples of a social studies program that promotes the attitudes and values essential to active and responsible citizenship in a democratic environment and that addresses the unique educational needs of early adolescents include the Civic Achievement Award Program (CAAP) (Close Up Foundation) and Learn–Serve projects to name just two. Although it is one of a number of examples of citizenship development programs, the authors believe it to be quite reflective of appropriate social studies curriculum for middle grades students. In this chapter, we provide an overview of this civic program for middle grades students.

Civic Achievement Award Program

From Knowledge, Skills, and Values to Practice

Civic literacy, citizenship competency, and citizen involvement are basic objectives of middle grades social studies education. Preparing middle grades students for citizenship is often discussed but not always carried out through specific citizenship development programs. The goal of the Civic Achievement Award Program (CAAP) is to turn words into action. The following description of CAAP is presented in a question-and-answer format and is adapted from CAAP publications.

1. What Is CAAP?

CAAP is a program designed to help students in grades 5 through 8 learn more about the United States and better understand what it means to be an American citizen. The program has three parts.

Part I—Learning Projects.   The Learning Project provides early adolescents with a common body of knowledge relating to U.S. history, geography, government, economics, culture, and current events. Interaction with these materials revolves around reading essays and completing various study sheets and a mastery test.

Part II—Research Project.   The Research Project provides early adolescents with the opportunity to locate and analyze information and communicate it to others. These skills are essential to active and responsible citizenship and are strengthened through gathering and processing information that is obtained from libraries and other sources of information.

Part III—Civic Project.   The Civic Project provides early adolescents with the opportunity to become informed and to develop opinions about civic issues. Students select an issue, identify alternatives for addressing it, assess the various consequences of such choices on themselves and others, and present their opinions on the issue in a public forum.

All participants are awarded a certificate for participating in CAAP. These certificates are included in the classroom materials. Participating teachers and schools also receive award certificates.

2. Who Can Participate?

All students in the fifth through eighth grades may participate in CAAP. The program is open to public, private, and parochial schools. Materials are part of a supplementary social studies program that may be used in a classroom, as a special program conducted by the school librarian, or as an afterschool program.

3. What Do Students Do in CAAP?

To participate in CAAP students follow a series of activities in a book prepared by the CAAP staff. The CAAP time line, essays, and study sheets guide students in learning, reviewing, and organizing basic information about the United States. Areas studied in the learning project are history, government, geography, economics, culture, and current events. After completing this portion of the program, students can take a mastery test to evaluate what they have learned. Directions on worksheets help students plan and conduct a research project. As a participatory experience, students engage in a civic project of their choice (and with their teacher's approval). Summary activities help students recognize how knowledge, skills, and participation are essential to active and responsible citizenship.

The CAAP provides numerous opportunities for middle grades students and teachers to establish a strong foundation for active and responsible citizenship. Incorporating teaching techniques appropriate to sound middle-level education, the program builds a knowledge and skills base essential to successful functioning in a democratic environment.

Reflecting on the objectives necessary to achieve effective citizenship, CAAP integrates knowledge from history, geography, and the other social sciences. At the same time, it provides developmentally appropriate educational experiences, enabling students to refine important intellectual-personal skills in a participatory framework, where knowledge and skills combine to promote the essential values, beliefs, and commitments.

Service Learning: Practice Makes Better Connections

The idea of connecting school learning with involvement in the wider community is not new. Increasingly, teachers have come to appreciate the inherent value of student involvement in the wider community as a planned part of the larger social studies curriculum. In recent years, national, state, and local efforts to involve students in various service activities in schools and communities and related community agencies have been funded by federal and state monies.

Service learning may be defined as an instructional approach that seeks to promote meaningful connections between curriculum content and community concerns and issues. Blending community service and classroom learning in a manner that enriches the educational, social, and personal development of early adolescents is the key to quality service learning.

Service learning is designed to meet existing community needs, should be coordinated between school and community, is integrated into each early adolescent's school-based academic curriculum, and provides students with myriad opportunities to use academic skills and knowledge in real-life circumstances in their communities. Finally, service learning is designed to enhance and expand what is taught in school by promoting learning beyond the classroom, and helps to foster a sense of caring for others (Alliance for Service Learning in Education Reform, 1993).

Outcomes of well-designed service learning include a deeper understanding of the obligations of active and responsible citizenship, improved communications, and problem-solving skills; enhanced self-esteem; and the addressing of concrete community-based needs. Given the complexity of such school–community connections, it is crucial to recognize reasonable standards in developing and executing service learning in the middle school. Specifically, effective service learning strengthens both service and academic learning and provides concrete opportunities for youngsters to learn new skills, to think critically, and to test new social-personal roles in the wider community. Preparation for and reflection on actual service-learning experience is crucial to the development of positive attitudes toward helping others. Finally, services performed must make a meaningful contribution to the community (Alliance for Service Learning in Education Reform, 1993).

While examples abound, the authors offer one example of service learning with which one of them was directly connected. The project, initiated by eighth-grade teachers at Wrens Middle School in Wren, Georgia, was titled "Beautifying WMS Campus." A description of that effort follows.

This beautification project was planned, developed, and brought to fruition by the teachers and students of the eighth grade at Wrens Middle School. It was designed to help students become more aware of environmental and ecological conditions around their school and throughout the local community. The project was interdisciplinary in that it combined studies in math, science, social studies, and language arts. Cooperative learning and life skills were also integrated into the unit.

All mainstreamed eighth graders participated in the project, both in the classroom and in the field. Students were encouraged but not required to participate in all phases of the project, allowing for individual preferences, interests, and abilities. One gratifying result of the project was a dramatic decline in severe discipline problems among a small group of students. Several students who heretofore had performed poorly in class did exceedingly well in the field, coordinating work schedules and performing much of the difficult labor associated with planting bed preparation.

The project was introduced by a visiting professional horticulturalist who brought potted plants, landscape blueprints, and a vast store of knowledge to share with students and teachers alike. This person was an engaging speaker and piqued the interest of students in a possible career choice. The language arts class researched plants, shrubs, and flowers indigenous to the climate of south Georgia. Differences among plants relative to degree of tolerance to direct sunlight were also studied. These data were utilized in math classes to design ideal gardens. After students measured the irregularly shaped garden plots, these measurements were used to determine square footage and related geometric designs. These activities led to ratio and proportion as related to scale drawings.

The science class used the scale drawings generated in math coupled with research data gathered in language arts class to determine which plants were appropriate, in light of such factors as shade/sunlight ratios at different times of the day, spacing requirements for different plant species, and general aesthetics of the area surrounding the garden plots. Social studies classes focused on the importance of service learning as it relates to self, family, school, and community. They next drew maps of Georgia and labeled the five physiographic regions, compared climate-weather patterns in each region, and produced booklets describing soil types and plant life in each region.

Following these and other classroom-based studies, students and teachers initiated the service component of the project. After planting plots were identified around the school, tilling began. Hard clay soil was loosened, removed, and replaced with rich soil appropriate for planting. The landscape design for each plot was also completed. These two activities were completed by various student–teacher teams, with students charged with the task of organizing and executing the work to everyone's satisfaction.

Following the planting of the several garden plots throughout the school grounds the continuing tasks of insect control, weeding, fertilizing, and watering were organized and assigned on a rotating basis. Interestingly, these students became very protective of their handiwork, assuring that no one trampled on their work or dropped litter on or around the plots. The school grounds looked appreciably better and this fact was recognized by both school and community leaders.

It is the hope of the teachers who organized and instituted this project that the idea will be expanded to include various areas of the local community, including the town square, various commercial areas in town, and such community places as the local elderly care facility. Finally, additional areas of the school campus will be improved through similar projects while maintaining those already planted (Liowns, McCants, Trepins, & Watkins, 1996).

THE MIDDLE-LEVEL CONNECTION: QUESTIONS TO PONDER

Before reflecting on and responding to these questions, secure a copy of your state's social studies guidelines. Given the view that social studies is concerned primarily with promoting active and responsible citizenship and that the curricular components essential to this end are knowledge, skills, values, and participation, the central questions are as follows:

For Preservice/Inservice Students
1. Do your state's social studies guidelines address this goal? If so, how? If not, what is missing?
2. Regardless of your response to Question 1, how might you promote active and responsible citizenship within the framework of your state's social studies program goals?
3. Does the knowledge base of your state's social studies guidelines include history, geography, the other social sciences, the humanities, and students' personal life experiences? If so, how is each addressed? If not, can you address such an absence in your school? At the state level? How?
4. Does the skills component of your state's social studies guidelines include those proposed in the "Report of the National Council for the Social Studies" (1989, pp. 384–385)? If so, how? If not, which skills are absent?
5. Does the values component of your state's social studies guidelines call for promotion of a coherent and consistent set of values for successful functioning in a democratic environment? If so, how? If not, how is the issue addressed?
6. Is there a civic or social participation component in your state's social studies guidelines? If so, will it truly promote active and responsible citizenship? How? If not, what can you do to overcome this situation?
7. What, if any, changes do you think should be made in your state's social studies guidelines? Assuming you list one or more changes, how might you play a role in fostering such changes?
8. What do you think of CAAP? Would it work in your school and with your students? Why or why not?

For Inservice Students
1. Do you currently provide students opportunities for civic or social participation in the community? If so, how do these compare to those of CAAP? If not, would you consider registering your students in CAAP? Explain your response.
2. Do you provide service-learning opportunities for your students? Explain your response.

FOOD FOR THOUGHT BEFORE MOVING ON

Take some time to compare your state's social studies guidelines with each of the recommendations offered in Chapter 1. General questions might include

1. Do your state's social studies guidelines reflect the recommendations offered in the first chapter? If so, how? If not, from which do they diverge?

2. Is it desirable that your state's social studies guidelines reflect "compatibility" with the recommendations offered in this publication? If not, which ones need not be reflected?
3. Where do you go from here to foster—and otherwise support and promote—improvement in your school's social studies program?

REFERENCES

Alliance for Service Learning in Education Reform. (1993).

"Designing a Social Studies Scope and Sequence for the 21st Century." (1986). *Social Education, 50*(7):484–542.

Liowns, A., F. McCants, J. Trepins, and T. Watkins. (1996). *Beautifying the WMS Campus: One Can Make a Difference*. Wrens, Georgia.

National Council for the Social Studies. (1990). *Social Studies Curriculum Planning Resources*. Dubuque, IA: Kendall/Hunt.

"Social Studies in the Middle School: A Report of the Task Force on Social Studies in the Middle School." (1991). *Social Education, 55*(5):287–293.

5

INSTRUCTION IN SOCIAL STUDIES

The Carnegie Council of Adolescent Development listed eight principles for a comprehensive middle school program in its report, *Turning Points: Preparing American Youth for the 21st Century.* In this chapter, we address Principle 2:

> Every student in the middle grades should learn to think critically through mastery of an appropriate body of knowledge, lead a healthy life, behave ethically and lawfully, and assume the responsibilities of citizenship in a pluralistic society.

SOME QUESTIONS

Preservice and inservice teachers require a method of instruction that enables students to actually participate in social studies. We suggest curriculum possibilities in which social studies content affords students the opportunity to learn about themselves and their community. The tension between the self (individual) and others (community) permits a host of learning experiences for understanding citizenship obligations better. An interesting way to proceed is to ask the following questions: "What is it to be civic-minded? What obligations does citizenship place on individuals? Does everyone in a Democracy need to participate?" (Parker, 1991, p. 4). Parker goes on to suggest two reasons for students to grapple with these questions. First, "such questions invite students to set off on historical adventures, the terrain and outcomes of which cannot be known in advance. These questions invite not just any adventures, but those that push us beyond our own experiences into a public world, into civility in all its forms" (p. 4). The second reason he proposes is judgment. It is the combination of historical understanding and judgment that enables individuals to make more informed decisions for themselves and their community.

In order to proceed to answer the questions Parker poses, we need to identify some broad organizing themes and focus our attention on them. The National Council of Social Studies (NCSS) 1991 Task Force on social studies instruction for middle-level students listed four unifying motifs in the social studies curriculum. We agree that these should be the basis of a good middle-level social studies program and provide the framework for understanding citizenship obligations:

1. Concern with self: development of self-esteem and a strong sense of identity
2. Concern for right and wrong: development of ethics
3. Concern for others: development of group and "other-centeredness"
4. Concern for the world: development of a global perspective

The practical problems middle school teachers face in attempting to achieve a synthesis between the egocentric (self) nature of students at this age and helping them to realize community responsibilities as reflected in the school's curriculum is no easy task. John Dewey recognized this problem. In his essay, *The Child and the Curriculum* (1902), he cited three areas that create problems between students and the curriculum: (1) the narrow but personal world of the child against the impersonal but infinitely extended world of time and space; (2) the unity, the single "wholeheartedness" of the child's life and the specialization and divisions of the curriculum; (3) the abstract principle of logical classification and arrangement and the practical and emotional bonds of child life.

ACTIVITIES

The activities we present attempt to bridge the world of the child, which is by definition immature and underdeveloped, to appreciate certain "social aims, meanings, and values incarnate in the matured experience of any adult" (Dewey, 1902, p. 2). The focus is the student who lives in a parochial world of immediate friends, family, and community, and who is not concerned with abstract concepts, facts, and laws; a Tom Sawyer, if you will. Teachers need to use the student's experience as a starting point for learning new material. "The child and the curriculum are simply two limits which define a single process" (Dewey, 1902). The activities we present are designed to achieve a synthesis between the world of the child and the values expressed in the school's curriculum.

In addition to our broad attempt to present activities that help develop active and responsible citizenship, we offer specific activities designed to meet the developmental needs of early adolescents. Because of its generative nature, each activity has many applications—from gifted programs to special needs students; from individual research topics to group projects; from self-contained classrooms moving toward a middle school approach to interdisciplinary teaching. We suggest ideas and possible directions—the teacher's imagination and resources determine the final form. Each activity

1. Is student-centered
2. Develops critical thinking skills
3. Reinforces writing skills
4. Provides opportunities for additional research and interdisciplinary learning
5. Promotes cooperative learning

Each of these elements is further discussed to include the most recent research and thinking in the field of middle-level education.

USING STUDENT-CENTERED ACTIVITIES

The activities we offer recognize the fact that students have different learning styles. As John M. Jenkins in *Learning Styles: Recognizing Individuality* (1991) writes,

> Terms like uniqueness, individual needs, and learning style have been part 'of the middle level education vocabulary, and learning process at this level and other levels of education can be described as an education involving student characteristics, teaching styles, and the learning environment without changing the other two factors. We look for the best way to teach groups of students rather than individuals. (p. 3)

The teacher's responsibility is to encourage the student to pursue various aspects of each activity that best correspond to his or her individual learning style. Learning preference can be determined by various instruments. The National Association of Secondary School Principals (NASSP) Learning Style Profile (LSP) provides student data on several elements of learning style.

- *Cognitive skill*—including analysis, spatial skills, discrimination, categorization, sequential processing, memory, and verbal-spatial preferences
- *Perceptional response*—including visual, auditory, and emotive
- *Study and instructional preferences*—such as persistence, study time, grouping, posture, mobility, temperature, lighting, and manipulative learning materials

Realizing the broad range of learning styles and abilities middle-school students possess, the authors developed and field-tested a variety of activities that accommodate many of the behaviors cited.

Developing Critical Thinking Skills

If we value thinking, then time should be spent in the classroom teaching thinking skills. The activities we offer are designed to reflect Bloom's Taxonomy of Educational Objectives (1956). Each activity provides possibilities to achieve a level of complex thinking. Although each of the activities presents a series of problems to be addressed, particular thinking can be taught to help students work more effectively toward a tentative solution.

The exact approach to teach thinking skills directly is not yet clear to many educators. There are currently three approaches under discussion and investigation today.

1. Teaching specific skills (e.g., comparing, classifying, or different forms of inferring based on the use of evidence) need to be defined, analyzed, and taught step by step.
2. Teaching thinking skills should be taught in a more nondirected holistic way.
3. If specific skills are diagnosed as being deficient or absent, remediation needs to occur to insure [sic] that autonomous thinking can take place. (Costa & Lowery, 1989, p. 77)

Until more research is compiled, the conflicts will persist. However, it seems to us that when a particular skill is necessary to solve a problem, it needs to be taught to students engaged in the activity.

Reinforcing Writing Skills

Social studies activities, like those presented in Part II, provide a framework for a variety of writing experiences. Writing a local history as a class project, a biographical sketch, a journal or diary, or a script for the News Show requires all the elements of good writing. Research activities allow students to experience the process of research and, at the same time, to develop a more critical eye toward research by others. Middle-level students need to be taught the process of good writing and research so they are better able to judge. Nancie Atwell (1990) suggests "that teachers of every discipline might ask students to think and write as scientists, historians, mathematicians, and literary critics do—to use writing as [a] process to discover meaning, just as these scholars do when they go about the real, messy business of thinking on paper" (p. xiii).

Through the writing process, students have an opportunity to explore areas other than their personal experiences. Struggling to reconcile conflicts presented by history, varying viewpoints, or personal decisions through writing forces deeper and complex thinking. "Now we understand that the most important part of the learning process comes during the writing while the student is struggling with ideas and with issues like form, audience, and voice" (Wilson, 1991).

Providing Opportunities for Additional Research and Interdisciplinary Learning

Areas of investigation in the social studies, which range from life on the Nile River in ancient Egypt to trying to understand man's balance with nature, by necessity involve interdisciplinary approaches. Interdisciplinary units or lessons involve the integration of several disciplines to help explain a particular concept. Beane (1990) offers the following example: "Imagine . . . a unit on identities in which students examine how self-perceptions are formed, how culture influences their self-concept, how various cultures express identities, and how increasing cultural diversity promises to reshape politics and the economy" (p. 11). In one of our activities, "Write Your Family History," many students will become interested in the economic, social, religious, and political forces that influenced their ancestors' decision to emigrate to America.

From unified arts to mathematics, most human problems cannot be adequately understood unless they are viewed through many lenses. Language arts help students present research in a coherent, concise way. Stretching middle-level students beyond a fixed curriculum into vicarious enjoyment of a particular time period through literature helps them understand and gain insight. Gayle Thieman (1992) offers yet another method: "Creating fictional journals can personalize for students the study of history and enable them to explain the lives of those often excluded, ordinary people. The journals serve as both windows into the past and as mirrors of students' own cultural heritage" (p. 185).

All of the activities suggested in the following section provide ample opportunities for interdisciplinary research. The teacher's role in the process is to act as coordinator. Students propose the areas of research that might interest them and proceed to investigate their aspect of the problem. Most often, the student's range of interest will create a natural interdisciplinary mode of inquiry.

Promoting Cooperative Learning

Jerry Rottier and Beverly Ogan's book, *Cooperative Learning in Middle-Level Schools* (1991), provides an excellent overview of the research in cooperative learning. The research on cooperative learning is extensive. For middle-level students, the following generalizations are significant.

Cooperative learning tends to promote higher achievement. This is especially true for average and slower students. Although cooperative learning has sometimes been criticized when used with bright students, it has been found that these students continue to receive high grades.

Cooperative learning promotes the greater use of reasoning strategies. When students are required to interact with one another, they improve their ability to become problem solvers. Students at the middle level who are just beginning to function at the abstract level will find their reasoning skills enhanced by participation in cooperative learning.

Cooperative learning promotes a positive relationship between students. This is especially valuable for middle-level students as they begin to interact with a wider range of students of both sexes.

Cooperative learning promotes more positive attitudes toward subject matter. Many middle-level students experience frustration as they interact independently with their subject matter. The ability to discuss the material with others can reduce this frustration and build a better relationship with the material being studied.

Cooperative learning promotes higher self-esteem. Developing positive relationships with other students and achieving a higher rate of success will help middle-level students improve their self-esteem.

Cooperative learning affords middle-level teachers opportunities to team-teach and create interdisciplinary activities. It is a method that provides the framework for specifying goals, content, knowledge, dispositions, values, behaviors, and skills to be learned.

Cooperate learning embodies many of the principles of a democratic society. As middle-level students begin to understand the relationship between individual rights and the responsibilities and obligations of citizenship, cooperative activities help them become aware of their role as future citizens. In 1988, R. Freeman Butts devised the Twelve Tables of Civism for the Modern American Republic (see Table 5-1). Many of the principles he proposed are consistent with elements found in cooperative learning strategies.

Freedom is one of the fundamental rights of citizenship:

The right, the opportunity, and the ability of every citizen to take an active part in shaping the institutions and laws under which he or she lives in common with others, and to do this by making uncoerced choices and by participating through active consent in cooperation with one's fellow citizens; and to do so in such a way as to

TABLE 5-1   Twelve Tables of Civism for the Modern American Republic
(with apologies to the "Laws of the Twelve Tables" of the
Early Roman Republic and to Aristotle's Paradigm of the Later
Greek Republics)

UNUM The Obligations of Citizenship		PLURIBUS The Rights of Citizenship	
Corrupted Forms of Unum	True Forms of Unum	True Forms of Pluribus	Corrupted Forms of Pluribus
"Law and order": enforced sameness; conformity	Justice; equality	Freedom; diversity	Anarchy; "unstable pluralism"
Authoritarianism; totalitarianism	Authority	Privacy	Privatism; privatization
"Majoritarianism"	Participation	Due process	"Soft on criminals"
"Beguiling half-truths"; plausible falsehood	Truth	Property	"Property rights superior to human rights"
Chauvinism; xenophobia	Patriotism	Human rights	"Cultural imperialism"
	Democratic civism		

promote justice, freedom, and equality for others. This is the freedom of the citizen and public action. (Butts, 1988, p. 242)

Cooperative activities promote skill development toward achieving this end. Rottier and Ogan (1991) list seven components of a cooperative learning lesson, in which we have included our observations.

1. *Face-to-face interaction.* Implied in this component is the principle of participation. Interaction is necessary and, therefore, students must be seated in ways that facilitate discussion. Small-group circles or desks that face one another are ways in which this can be accomplished.

2. *Evaluation.* Each person is held accountable to master specific objectives of the lesson. It might be vocabulary words, map skills, historical knowledge based on research, understanding an economic principle, or a temperature chart. The overall group evaluation is a composite of each individual contribution.

3. *Individual accountability.* Each individual is responsible for the overall performance of the group. Teachers need to be aware that each individual has mastered specific skills. This mastery toward a group end helps students realize their obligation in society.

4. *Group cohesion.* As students work together toward developing a team effort, part of the learning experience will include the struggle between the principle of equality and its corrupted form, conformity. Middle-level students are easily coerced into "going along with the group" at the expense of individual conscience.

5. *Social skills development.* A whole series of skills can be learned employing a cooperative lesson. Presenting an idea, accepting a different viewpoint, staying on task, maintaining an acceptable level of noise, problem solving, and leadership responsibilities are all elements that enable students to become effective group participants. Groups should be structured according to academic, race, and gender differences, to support the principle of diversity.

6. *Monitoring.* Teachers need to know if students are achieving intellectual development in cooperative activities. Objectives and skill competencies need to be clearly stated before the lesson begins. Charts, time frames, checklists, portfolio assessments, and so on will aid the teacher in determining student progress.

7. *Processing.* At the completion of each cooperative activity, students need to have an opportunity to discuss their progress. It is critical that students receive this feedback on both positive contributions and areas that need improvement.

Citizenship Education

William T. Callahan, in the introduction to *Citizenship for the 21st Century* (1990), writes, "In order to cope with the demands of modern citizenship, students need a broad general introduction to civic life—they need a curriculum that provides them with key knowledge content from a variety of disciplines, basic civic skills and competencies, and an understanding of the democratic principles and citizenship responsibilities."

Recently, in our society, many have expressed concern that the republic is in cardiac arrest. Voter apathy is but the tip of the iceberg. Critics of the 1970s and 1980s have suggested that individualism at the expense of the community has ravaged America. Lasch's (1978) concept of a narcissistic, inner-directed culture, and political and economic scandals—Watergate, Irangate, Wall Street trading, and the plight of the savings and loan system—all serve to support the notion that we, as a people, have relinquished our obligations as citizens.

The challenge is to restore that fragile balance between the private domain and the public obligations of a citizen. Two concepts emerge when wrestling with this problem, justice and virtue. Although classical in origin they are very important today. The assumption is that if a society is composed of just citizens, then justice will prevail at all levels of society, and justice will be the standard by which to judge all decisions.

Of virtue, James Madison wrote in 1787, "I go on this great republican principle, that people will have virtue and intelligence to select men of virtue and wisdom. Is there no virtue among us? To suppose that any form of government will secure liberty or happiness without any virtue in the people is an absurd idea."

Michael Hartoonian (1990) reminds us that "the notion that common individuals could be reservoirs of virtue, as opposed to virtue being vested in a King or the aristocracy, was and may still be a radical political concept" (p. 262).

As we discussed in Chapter 2, one of the four models used in teaching social studies is social studies as citizenship transmission. Edward Miller (1988) in his paper, "An Assessment of College Civic Literacy," comments that civic education has a multitude of meanings. State statutes do not define civic education in value-neutral terms. Patriotism, devotion to America, and principles of democracy are included in the laws that govern civic education. We would argue that, done well, this is a political socialization model aimed at integrating students into the "civic mainstream" of American life.

A second model holds that civic education is knowledge of the political. Typically, this includes factual knowledge of the Constitution, political processes, including the relationship among levels of government, and public policy. "One advantage of this approach is that those individuals who are more knowledgeable tend to be more efficacious, and those more efficacious tend to participate at a greater rate in conventional political participatory activities such as voting" (Cleary, 1971; Nie, Verba, & Petrocik, 1976). The implications are clear for middle-level educators. Greater knowledge enhanced by content is a precondition of participatory democracy. However, sheer content at the factual level—Bloom's notion of lower level learning objectives—does not necessarily lead to higher levels of thinking.

A third view of civic education sees civic competence as analytical ability, a capability to dissect arguments and validate positions. "Among political systems, democracy is viewed as unique for the burden it puts on its citizens to be active, informed, and capable of rendering judgments" (p. 4). Thus, critical thinking activities introduced to middle-level students are an essential function of political education.

Cherryholmes (1981) presents yet a fourth view of civic education that is consistent with our own. Civic competency can be regarded as a social science whose behavioral and political sciences are emphasized more than the sum of constitutions, structures, descriptions, and history. Miller (1988) writes, "The social science orientation incorporates the analytical approach to political questions, but extends to include social scientific methods of inquiry" (p. 40).

The intent of Chapters 4, 5, and 6 is to provide teachers with activities and extensions that will help middle-level students begin to develop critical abilities for solving today's challenges. Students will come to appreciate the need for a historical, present, and future perspective, as they wrestle with issues that will affect them. Richard E. Neustadt and Ernest R. May in *Thinking in Time* (1986) succinctly state our goals:

> To link conventional wisdoms of the present with past counterparts and future possibilities; to link interpretations of the past with experiences of interpreters, and both with prescriptions; to link proposals for the future with the inhibitions of the present as inheritances from the past—all these mean to think relatively and in terms of time, opening one's mind to possibilities as far back as the story's start and to potentialities as far ahead as relevant (judged, or course, from now, hence subject to revision later). (p. 246)

We believe that the additional activities that follow will engage students, promote skill development, develop critical thinking, and build the social and intellectual foundations for active and responsible citizenship.

When a teacher combines cooperative learning with citizenship education, several goals are achieved. The activity, "Protect That Source: A Mock Trial," gives students an opportunity to work in cooperative groups (defense team, prosecution team, and jury) and at the same time begin to develop an understanding of civic values as the conflict between the First and Sixth Amendments is debated.

PROTECT THAT SOURCE: A MOCK TRIAL

"Order in the court!" the judge bellows as he pounds the gavel three times. The classroom is transformed into a courtroom. The defendants and the plaintiff eagerly wait to be called to the witness stand. Lawyers pencil in last-minute notes in preparation for their oral arguments and stinging cross-examinations. The jury is poised, ready to listen to all the evidence. The trial begins.

A mock trial turns seemingly ponderous pages of dust-covered legal briefs, unintelligible to most readers, into an exciting encounter, not only with the U.S. Constitution but also with the legal and law enforcement community. This particular case addresses another compelling problem: drug abuse.

This court activity addresses the "freedom of press" clause in the First Amendment. Currently, there are two heated and related journalists' issues under discussion. The question of a newsperson's privilege in court is connected to the question raised in the *Stanford Daily* case (*Zurcher v. The Stanford Daily*, 1978) of the sanctity of a newsroom and its files, where most of the confidential information is kept. The topic of journalistic privilege is chosen because it implicitly includes many of the newsroom arguments, it has able advocates on both sides of the issue, and it has a long history of courtroom dispute.

Also relevant to this activity on journalists' privilege are the recent state and federal court decisions in which freedom of the press seemed to be at odds with other constitutional guarantees, as well as other public interests, such as effective law enforcement.

There are two major reasons for doing a courtroom activity on journalists' privilege. First, to discuss the role of the press in maintaining a democratic society and, second, to illustrate that the preservation of a reasonably stable society is the constant balancing of competing rights and interests. This activity addresses the following concepts: balancing of interests, confidentiality, fair trial, freedom of the press, journalistic ethics, and journalists' privilege.

The Problem

A reporter refuses to disclose his source to the court in a trial that involves local drug activity. In this case, the source is a contact in the local drug ring. The reporter has written several prize-winning articles on drugs in the local community and plans to use the same source for information on other activities linked to organized crime. The plaintiff (the state) is in court claiming that the defendant (the reporter), by refusing to disclose the source, is preventing the state from performing its duties of protecting citizens from illegal activities. Does the reporter have the right not to disclose the source to the state?

This activity provides an opportunity to teach basic constitutional concepts, drug awareness, and judicial procedure. It needs to be broken down into four separate teaching components: preparation; community speakers; courtroom procedure; and the student's mock trial.

Preparation

When the court activity is introduced, students will want to hold court immediately. Unfortunately, in order to achieve a successful trial, they must be knowledgeable of the issues in the case, recent court decisions, and legal definitions (vocabulary). The initial phase is their preparation. The following section is based on "Should Journalists Have the Right to Protect Their Sources?" in *A Teachers Guide to the Advocates* (Smith, 1979, pp. 6–8).

At this point, the materials used for the activity are presented in the following manner. All students will review the sections that include copies of the First Amendment, the Sixth Amendment, vocabulary, and terms. The class is then divided into three groups, the Plaintiff (the state), the Defendant (the reporter), and the jury. Sworn to secrecy, the plaintiff and the defendant will receive additional information that includes three recent court cases and three basic arguments that will support their position.

Vocabulary

Abridging	Dissidents	Shield laws
Anonymous	Due process	Sixth Amendment
Branzburg v. Hayes	First Amendment	Sources
Bureaucratic	Grand jury	Statute
Censorship	Journalistic ethics	Subpoena
"Chilling"	Journalists' privilege	*The New York Times Company*
Circumvent	Press	*and Myron Farber v. Mario*
Compulsory	Prior restraint	*E. Jascalevich*
Confidential	Search warrant	*Zurcher v. The Stanford Daily*

Defendant's witness #1: presents testimony; cross-examination by plaintiff's lawyer.

This format continues until all the witnesses have had an opportunity to present their arguments. Witnesses may be recalled to the stand for further interrogation.

Student Mock Trial

This is the day everyone has been waiting for. The classroom is transformed into a courtroom. Let students create their own setting. They are always true to form.

A Sample Cast of Characters

Judge: the classroom teacher. Order must be maintained and legal disputes resolved.

Two to three attorneys for the plaintiff.

Two to three attorneys for the defendant.

Witnesses for the plaintiff: police officer; FBI agent; undercover agent; legal scholar; drug counselor; former addict.

Witnesses for the defendant: reporter; CBS anchorperson; legal scholar; editor of *The New York Times*; "60 Minutes" reporter.

Court stenographer: takes actual notes or tape records.

Officer of the court.

Jury

Reference

Smith, Douglas. (1979). "Should Journalists Have the Right to Protect Their Source?" In *A Teacher's Guide to the Advocates*. Boston: WGBH Educational Foundation.

ADOPTING A GLOBAL PERSPECTIVE

How then does a middle grades teacher attempt to achieve such goals in the social studies? To many, social studies at first appears as a vast forest, incomprehensible, a tangled undergrowth of intertwining disciplines, each competing for its own space. To both student and teacher, it can be confusing. Like a meadow splashed with myriad colors, many species, and multiple fragrances, it displays an ordered chaos whose nature can only be appreciated when its patterns are understood.

Two areas are discussed to answer these questions. The traditional geography metaphor of "earth as home" is expanded to include all the social studies. The concept of citizenship education is expanded to incorporate the relationship between the individual and the community. This discussion is designed to place the critical thinking activities that follow into a practical context.

A medieval view of the world suggested that it was chaotic, dangerous, corrupt, and disease-ridden and that the only salvation or remedy was heaven, that celestial body of perfection just beyond the moon. The earth was both physically and spiritually inhospitable to humanity. Today, by contrast, we look to the earth as a nurturing place floating in a cold black void between incalculable other celestial bodies. Shakespeare's image of England offers a parallel to our view of Earth today.

> This precious stone set in a silver sea,
> Which serves it in the office of a wall,
> Or as a mat defensive to a house
> Against the envy of less happier lands;
> This blessed plot, this earth, this realm
> *Richard II*

So today "earth as home of humanity" seems an appropriate metaphor. We have no place else to go. The physical frontiers no longer exist. Space exploration promises opportunities for better understanding of the world but offers little in terms of extended human habitation. Earth is our only natural refuge. To exist together as a global community is one of this generation's greatest challenges.

We need to teach students how to employ the social science disciplines to understand how to achieve such a lofty goal. Our survival may well depend on it. Dewey wrote, in speaking of history and geography as subject matter, that "it is to enrich and liberate the most direct and personal contacts of life by furnishing their context, their background, and outlook" (Dewey, 1902, p. 211). This argument can be easily expanded to include the other social science disciplines as well. More recently, the National Council for Geographic Education and the American Association of Geographers (*Guidelines for Geographic Education*, 1984) developed five basic themes as organizers to help students understand geography. These are

1. location
2. place
3. region
4. human–environment interactions
5. movement

These five basic themes may be used to help students understand the context, background, and outlook of most problems encountered in social studies. As a mode of scientific inquiry, these themes provide an effective method for asking questions about places and people's relationship to those places in a historical, contemporary, and future context. It involves a pattern of inquiry that begins with two essential questions: Why are such things located in those particular places, and, How do those particular places influence our lives? (*Guidelines for Geographic Education*, 1984).

Absolute and Relative Location

All events take place somewhere. *Absolute* location is a precise point on the earth. *Relative* location places absolute locations in relation to one another. An example is oil reserves in the Persian Gulf. Were the Suez Canal not close to oil deposits in the Middle East, the price of oil in Western Europe would increase significantly because of additional shipping costs around southern Africa.

Place

Place implies human characteristics, physical characteristics, and environmental perception. Many of the social sciences can be used to understand place. Economists and demographers help us understand economic activities and settlement patterns. Anthropologists and sociologists offer insights into cultural patterns. Theologians, political scientists, and philosophers often address the issue of ideology. The simple question "Where is a good place to live?" is an excellent starting point to find out just how many disciplines are required to answer it.

Region

Regions imply areas exhibiting common characteristics. It could mean climatic, crop, or political areas. The Corn Belt, Dairy Belt, Sun Belt, Pacific Rim, and Gold Coast are examples of regions best understood through different social sciences. Another advantage of using regions is that students can create their own regions by incorporating physical or human characteristics they feel are common to a particular area.

Human–Environment Interactions

The study of *human–environment interactions* presents people's most basic problem—adapting to their environment or adapting the environment to fit their needs. This encompasses adapting to harsh environments, environmental determinism, environmental modification (agriculture, industry, global warming, rain forests), man-made hazards such as nuclear disasters, oil spills, thermal pollution, and population growth.

Movement

Movement includes the interplay of people, products, and ideas—for example, emigration and immigration; voyages of discovery, rediscovery, or exploration; transportation and foreign trade; capitalism, communism, and socialism; religious fundamentalism; and global interdependence.

Any time a problem or issue is investigated, you can use one or more of the five themes as a frame of reference to help students understand the problem. In addition, you can also use whichever of the social science disciplines is needed to comprehend the problem. Because they all interact, they are like a symphony. When one theme dominates, the others play in the background. Hence, a useful way to teach the social studies is to incorporate the five themes as a way of helping students organize their thinking about problems. The metaphor "Earth as the home of humanity" and the five basic themes provide an excellent way of thinking, and they easily correlate with Bloom's Taxonomy of Learning Objectives (1956). For example:

Evaluation	↔	Region
Synthesis	↔	Movement
Analysis	↔	Human–environment interaction
Application	↔	Place

Interpretation   ↔   Location

Comprehension   ↔   Basic geographic facts

WHOSE VIEW OF THE WORLD?
MAPS AND THEIR USES

A map is worth a thousand words. It explains and shows not only how to get there from here, but also what one can expect along the way. *Cartographical Innovations: An International Handbook of Mapping Terms to 1900* (Wallis and Robinson, 1987) lists 191 different entries consisting of eight specific groups of maps.

1. Types of maps
2. Maps of human occupations and activities
3. Maps of natural phenomena
4. Reference systems and geodetic concepts
5. Symbolism
6. Techniques and media
7. Methods of duplication
8. Atlases

Each type and specific map furnishes the user with great detail, enabling students to better understand information not provided in any other format. In spite of the immense variety of maps, the central concept middle schoolers will learn is that all maps are symbolic representations of a particular worldview. This view is affected by cultural attitudes and technology. Although similarities exist among maps, cultural differences give each map its unique distinctiveness.

Map activities will help middle schoolers learn basic map skills and reinforce the five basic themes.

1. *Location.* Probably the most obvious use of maps. Absolute and relative locations can easily be seen by using maps and the globe. Distance between locations helps students develop an awareness of time and distance, whether for an early explorer attempting to circumnavigate the globe or for a family vacation from Seattle, Washington, to Mesa Verde, Colorado.

2. *Place.* Topographical maps reveal where we are—on a plain, a hill, or a mountain. Climatic maps suggest data concerning temperature and precipitation. Population maps indicate the density of people living in specific areas and at particular times. Using the three maps used in the following sections, students can develop hypotheses about specific places. What kind of

place is it? Would I like to live there? What can be done to make it a better place to live? Is it possible? All of these questions ask what the human and physical characteristics of the place are.

3. *Region.* Maps can help students identify and create regions. Middle schoolers find characteristics common to an area and pinpoint a region. The Corn Belt, Rust Belt, Dairy Belt, and Pacific Rim are a few examples of well-known regions. However, investigative minds can create new regions. Students can identify regional characteristics where religion, language, economic activity, climate, river systems, rail lines, and so forth intersect.

4. *Human–environment interaction.* What happens when people migrate into a previously unsettled area? If trees are cut and farms developed, how does that affect the environment? Or conversely, what happens when people decide to reforest an area? From the earliest civilizations along major river systems to our present densely populated centers of trade and commerce humans have had an impact on the environment. At what cost? The fragile balance between human settlement and the health of our natural environment is a major concern as we move toward the twenty-first century. Maps provide students with problem-solving activities that will enable them to suggest and predict possible future outcomes. What have we learned from the poor farming practices of the 1930s that created the "Dust Bowl"? Is deforestation in Brazil going to create similar conditions in Latin America, as might the unprecedented harvesting of old-growth forests in America's Northwest? What are the economic and ethical questions raised by human development? Time lines and maps aid in the comprehension of such complex problems. They can demonstrate the impact human activity has on the environment and promote a new way of thinking about the future.

5. *Movement.* Migrations of peoples can be easily understood by middle-level students when they are visually represented. Movement allows students to investigate the push-pull factors that are responsible for population displacement. Movement is not only a human condition, but it also includes physical elements in the environment. The slow but relentless movement of the Sahara Desert in Northern Africa is creating problems for which solutions need to be found. Shorelines in coastal zones are also affected by the movement of the oceans. The extent to which these conditions affect human populations is another set of problems that students can analyze.

The purpose of the next section is to show middle-level teachers three map activities that can help their students develop critical thinking skills. The first activity is designed to teach the concept of distortion by using several historical and cross-cultural maps. The second focuses on the Salem Witchcraft Trials, which are fundamental to understanding conformity, order, and obedience. In addition to the way the trials have been explained historically and portrayed by Arthur Miller's *The Crucible*, another approach is to use maps to show the community relationships that were the source of the problem.

Distortion Map Activity

The use of distortion is a difficult concept for most middle schoolers to grasp. One way to help them understand it is to offer them the chance to create their own maps. In the process of working with distortion problems, they will better understand it. This activity is divided into three sections: (1) local community and grid; (2) overview of historical and cross-cultural maps; and (3) students as cartographers.

Materials and Location

Use paper on large rolls. Paper can be obtained from local paper companies or distributors. Use color markers, paint, masking tape, line, scissors, and so on. Because of the space required, we suggest a basement, storage area, or annex. If the project is combined with a unified arts program, use the art room.

Community Map and Grid

First, let students spend time studying their own community by using a local map. Basic concepts, such as the scale, legend, and symbols, can be reviewed or learned. The amount of time required will depend on students' previous experience and knowledge. Give an explanation of a grid. Here is an opportunity to use some basic math computations. Superimpose a grid over the community map. This becomes the basis for enlarging or reducing the student's map. Explain about the origins of grids.

> The square grid originated in China in the first century when the famous astronomer Chang Heng cast a network about heaven and earth and reckoned on the base of it. The rectangular grid was in continuous use in China from the time of Phei Hsiu to the late sixteenth century when the European missionaries arrived in China. The Yu Chi Thu, 1137, is one of the notable examples of a grid map. In the Western world the square grid was used in Greek and Roman surveying and then seems to have disappeared, emerging in the maps of the Holy Land made by Pietro Vesconte in Venice, c. 1327. It has been suggested that travelers to the east may have brought back information on the Chinese grid. The Franciscan William of Ruback, for example, on his travels to Mongolia, 1251–1254, learned details of Chinese or Korean maps from the Mongols which he passed on to Vincent de Beauvais and Roger Bacon. Marco Polo returned from China to Venice in 1295 with maps

whose details were incorporated into the Catalan map of 1375. Square grids are also found in twelfth-century medieval copies of Roman surveying manuals from about 50 A.D. (Wallis & Robinson, 1987, XII)

From first-century Chinese grids to twentieth-century middle school grids, the basic principles remain the same. Invite students to use different scales for the same map so they can visualize the advantages of different scales. What information can be obtained from a scale that is 1 inch equals 100 miles (1 in. = 100 mi) compared to one that is 1 inch equals 10 miles (1 in. = 10 mi)? Once students are proficient in using grids, the next step is to introduce them to a variety of historical and cross-cultural maps.

Overview of Historical and Cultural Maps

Devote several lessons to showing and explaining several historical maps. The ones in this chapter can be found in *Cartographical Innovations*, and most libraries are shelved with atlases, gazetteers, and reference materials. After the lessons, students will be able to use basic cartographic principles to create their own maps in ways that reflect a historical time period or a different world view by drawing their own community. The following examples are offered as possibilities; however, given the vast number of maps available, middle school teachers should develop their own map problem-solving activities. Once students have learned about route maps, T-O maps, and subway maps, they will be ready to reproduce their own maps.

Route Map

Route maps are probably the oldest maps known. They are simply a strip in which routes between places are marked, usually to indicate distance. As Wallis and Robinson (1987) point out, "people in every culture from the earliest times have shown an instinctive ability to express distance, often in units of time such as a day's journey, and direction, established from observations of the sun and movement of the stars" (p. 57).

In Egypt, copies of the "Book of the Two Ways," describing the journey of the departed soul in the afterlife, have been found in coffins. Long Chinese scrolls dating from the first century reflect the great importance of rivers to the economy. The Romans as early as the second century also used scrolls on which maps were scribed. During the fourth and fifth centuries, the Peutinger Table comprised a road map of the entire Roman Empire on a long strip (scroll) 1 ft × 25 ft. More recently, a North American Indian birch bark route map was found in 1841 attached to a tree between Lake Huron and the Ottawa River in upper Canada (see Map 5-1).

Map 5-1

Roman Military Map

The Romans conquered the ancient world. How did they know how to send the Roman Legions to Gaul and Britannia? Maps, of course! In the spirit of Roman military cartographers, assign 4 to 5 students to draw their own community using the Peutinger Table as a model (see Map 5-2). The map (scroll) will be 1 ft × 25 ft. Use the community grid, and distort it to accommodate the new map. A helpful aid in teaching the concept of distortion is to make an impression with silly putty and then stretch it. When the community map is redrawn to conform to the Peutinger Table, it will wrap around the classroom like a ribbon. This is a challenging cooperative group activity.

T-O Map

The T-O map is one of the two types of mappa mundi made in the period from the fifth to the tenth centuries (see Map 5-3). "The term *mappa mundi* was used for medieval (usually circular) world maps, made between the fall of the western Roman empire in the late years of the fifth century A.D. and the end of the fifteenth century. The Latin word 'mappa' means patch, napkin, or cloth" (Wallis & Robinson, 1987, p. 87). T-O maps were oriented with east at the top. One of the examples we have used was found in a German cathedral. Located on the floor of the church, the mosaic tile map, 12 feet in diameter, had Jerusalem at the center. The O represents the oecumene and the T, the axis of the Mediterranean crossed by the meridian from the Don to the Nile. Students placed their school at the center of their map and, once again, using grid, distorted the rest of their community to conform to the mappi mundi. Although large rolls of paper taped together and then cut in a 12-foot circle are useful, it is not inconceivable to patch together cloth to achieve the same effect and be consistent with the original maps.

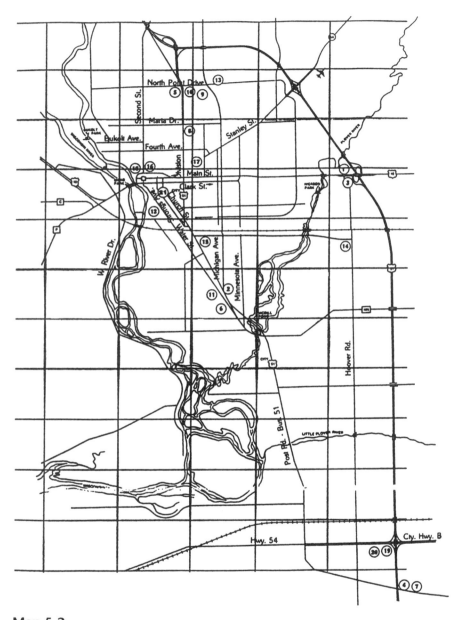

Map 5-2

Map 5-3

Subway Map

As population increases and urban areas expand, efficient mass transit becomes a problem. Almost all large urban centers in the world today provide some form of transportation to and from the hub of economic activity. Another intriguing problem for middle-level students is to design a subway map that will reflect the needs of their community. The number of stops and where they are are important considerations. Where is the population density the highest, and where is it in relation to the business district? Where are the greatest number of people employed, and where do they live? Once basic data have been collected, then preliminary routes can be drawn. At this point, other problems present themselves. What construction problems exist? How will they traverse rivers, hills, and existing buildings? Do they travel under the ground or above the ground?

This activity helps students think not only about problems of design and scale but also about future community planning.

The previous map activities help students understand the process involved in creating maps. Maps are also used to explain events. The Salem witchcraft episode provides a different type of critical thinking approach.

Salem Witchcraft Trials

In 1692 a devastating explosion of hysteria ripped the very fabric of Salem village. Adolescent girls accused local citizens of practicing witchcraft. This led to the execution of 19 innocent people and the imprisonment of 150 more. What actually happened and the reason for it have been the subjects of research by historians and writers. We find two stories extremely useful in helping students to understand this time period; *The Crucible*, a play by Arthur Miller, and an analysis, *Salem Possessed: The Social Origins of Witchcraft* (1974) by Paul Boyer and Stephen Nissenbaum.

In concert with performing *The Crucible* or particular scenes from it, it is also helpful to present a series of maps so students can better understand community relationships. The following maps are adaptations from *Salem Possessed*.

A brief history is in order to fully understand the dimensions of the 1692 accusations. In 1672, Salem Village was granted the right to establish a church. For years, it had petitioned the General Court for this status. Like many New England towns, most people wanted to separate from bigger communities and obtain permission to hire their own ministers because of the great distances they had to travel to meeting houses. In Salem, the distance was not only in terms of actual miles but also, more important, a distance between two value systems. Salem Village geographically was inland and agricultural, reflecting conventional values of the times. Ideas and changes were slow to affect the lives of Salem villagers. On the other hand, Salem Town established mercantile ties with London and the Caribbean. Ideas were disseminated quickly. The profits from trade changed the lives of the inhabitants at Salem Town, and the gulf between village and town began to widen (see Map 5-4).

Though political boundaries suggest the similarity of interests (states, nation, etc.), these are never clear-cut. A second look at Salem Village in 1692 reveals an interesting pattern. Ask students to determine any pattern that might exist (see Map 5-5). Students will see that Salem Village is almost divided in half regarding the witchcraft accusations. It is interesting to note that the accused witches and their defenders live closest to Salem Town and the ocean. Do witches and their defenders prefer larger towns and the ocean? Or are there other explanations? Other maps will be needed to help students answer this question.

The tempest that struck in 1692 moved through the community like a hurricane, expanding and gradually uprooting all aspects of early colonial village life. The accusations moved from the center at Salem Village to include persons as far away as Boston. The initial conflict stemmed from the debate over hiring Samuel Parris as minister of Salem Village in 1689. Internal village bickering and squabbling over the terms of his contract, property, and even over the amount of wood he was provided sowed the seeds of destruction.

Two maps illustrate the residential patterns that existed just before and after the witchcraft accusations. Two prominent Salem families, the Porters and the Putnams, were involved in the dispute of Samuel Parris and the witchcraft accusations. (For a complete analysis, see Boyer & Nissenbaum, 1974, pp. 110–137.) Each with almost identical histories, families, and landholdings found themselves in opposite camps (see Map 5-6).

Salem: Town and Village

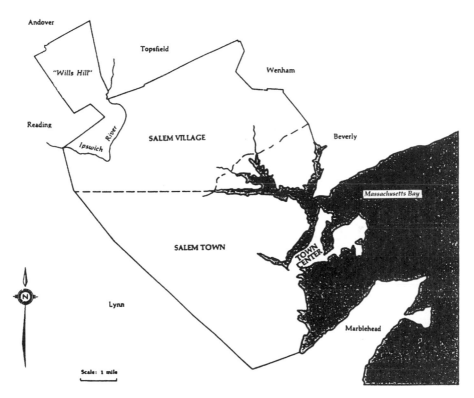

Map 5-4

At this point, present Map 5-6. Ask students to compare Map 5-5 with Map 5-6. What are their conclusions? Is there any relationship between Porter property and the witchcraft accusations? Are the defenders of the witches Porters or persons sympathetic to the Porters? What motives might the Putnams have to accuse people of witchcraft? Are these people actual witches who are being accused?

After the trials, imprisonments, and executions, the hysteria finally subsided, bringing in its wake some interesting geographical patterns: "In April 1695 an ecclesiastical council meeting at Salem Village, under the leadership of the Reverend Increase Mather, hints that Parris should resign; eighty-four of Parris's Village opponents petition the council members to take a stronger stand" (Boyer & Nissenbaum, 1974, p. xvii). The council members in May recommended more forcibly that Parris resign; one hundred five of Parris's village supporters sign a petition in his behalf. The Salem Village Church endorsed Parris in June who served to remain as minister until the following July 1696 when

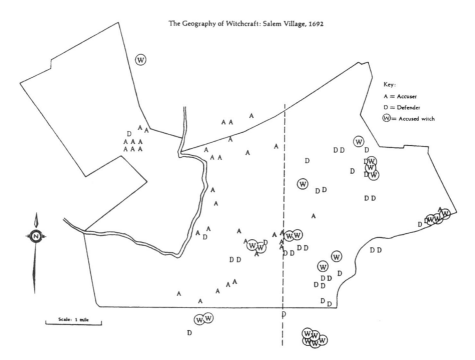

Map 5-5

he resigned. Throughout the pro-Parris and anti-Parris petitions of 1695, it is interesting to note where the supporters of each faction resided.

On Map 5-7 ask students to count the number of pro-Parris and anti-Parris supporters in the section that is marked off by dashed lines. What conclusions do they draw from this analysis?

Maps 5-4 through 5-7 help students understand some of the aspects of a very complex social problem. It is clear that geographical patterns begin to shed light on the witchcraft hysteria. In addition, other questions for further research should be considered. Which individual people were accused? Initially, women who were considered deviants or outcasts in the community: Tituba, the West Indian slave, Sarah Good, a pauper, and "Gamma Osborne," a bedridden old woman. As the accusations increased, a broader range of villagers were included, though one pattern remains clear: People opposed to the Reverend Parris were the subject of accusations.

Reference

Boyer, Paul, and Stephen Nissenbaum. (1974). *Salem Possessed: The Social Origins of Witchcraft*. Cambridge, MA: Harvard University Press.

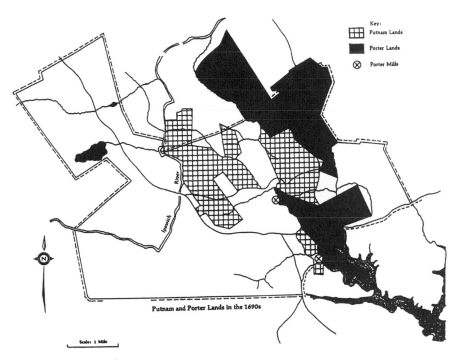

Key:
Putnam Lands
Porter Lands
⊗ Porter Mills

Putnam and Porter Lands in the 1690s

Scale: 1 Mile

Map 5-6

REFERENCES

Atwell, Nancie, ed. (1990). *Coming to Know: Writing to Learn in the Intermediate Grades.* Portsmouth, NH: (1990).

Beane, James. (1990). *A Middle School Curriculum: From Rhetoric to Reading.* Columbus, OH: National Middle School Association.

Bloom, Benjamin S. (1956). *Taxonomy of Educational Objectives.* New York: Longmors, Green.

Butts, R. Freeman. (1988). *The Morality of Democratic Citizenship: Goals for Civic Education in the Republic's Third Century.* Calabasas, CA: Center for Civic Education.

Callahan, William, ed. (1990). *Citizenship for the 21st Century.* Foundation for Teaching Economics.

Cherryholmes, C. (1981). "U.S. Social and Political Education." *Teaching Political Science,* 8:245–260.

Cleary, R. E. (1971). *Political Education and American Democracy.* Scranton, PA: InText Educational Publishers.

Costa, Arthur L., and Lawrence F. Lowery. (1989). *Techniques for Teaching Thinking.* Pacific Grove, CA: Midwest Publications.

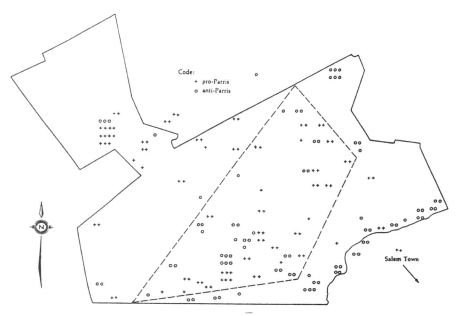

The Geography of Factionalism: Residential Pattern
of the Signers of the Pro-Parris and Anti-Parris
Petitions of 1695

Map 5-7

Dewey, John. (1902). *The Child and the Curriculum.* Chicago: University of Chicago Press.

Federalist Papers. (1961). "A commentary on the Constitution of the United States, being a collection of essays written in support of the Constitution agreed upon September 17, 1787, by the Federal Convention from the original text of Alexander Hamilton, John Jay, and James Madison." New York: Modern Library.

Guidelines for Geographic Education. (1984). Joint Committee on Geographic Education of the National Council for Geographic Education and Association of American Geographers.

Hartoonian, Michael. (1990). Unpublished manuscript, Wisconsin Council of Social Studies, Madison.

Jenkins, John M. (1991). "Learning Styles: Recognizing Individuality." *Schools in the Middle.*

Lasch, Christopher. (1978). *The Culture of Narcissism: American Life in an Age of Diminishing Expectations.* New York: Norton.

Miller, Edward. (1988). "An Assessment of College Civic Literacy." *College Student Journal,* 2–12.

Neustadt, Richard E., and Ernest R. May. (1986). *Thinking in Time*. New York: The Free Press.

Nie, N.N., S. Verba, and J.R. Petrocik. (1976). *The Changing American Voter*. Cambridge, MA: Harvard University Press.

Parker, William C. (1991). *Reviewing the Social Studies Curriculum*. Alexandria, VA: Association for Supervision and Curriculum Development.

Rottier, Jerry, and Beverly J. Ogan. (1991). *Cooperative Learning in Middle-Level Schools*. Washington, DC: National Education Association.

Thieman, Gayle Y. (1992). "Using Fictional Journals to Study Underrepresented Groups in History." *Social Education, 5*(3):185–186.

Wallis, Helen M., and Arthur H. Robinson, eds. (1987). *Cartographical Innovations: An International Handbook of Mapping Terms to 1900*. Tring, England: Map Collector Publications in Association with the International Carteographic Association.

Wilson, David E. (1991). "Teaching Writing: Middle Level Teachers Change Their Focus." *Schools in the Middle*.

6

CRITICAL THINKING ACTIVITIES

Chapter 6 is designed to help teachers develop appropriate instructional activities for students which lead to the development of critical thinking skills. Though generic in nature each of the activities presents background materials and suggestions for how to use it. Units of instruction and lesson planning are easily adapted to specific classroom settings from the activities.

ACTIVITIES FORMAT

Example.   Oil: Implications for Global Interdependency (see pp. 134–143)

Goal.   Asked in the form of a general question. To what extent is the future of a democratic society tied to a stable oil market?
What key terms or concepts need to be taught to achieve the goal?

Key Terms/Concepts

alliance	inexhaustible resource	recession
alternative source	inflation	renewable resource
colonialism	interdependence	resource depletion
consumption	nationalism	scarcity
dependence	nonrenewable resource	self-sufficiency
depletion	OPEC	supply and demand
fossil fuel	opportunity costs	

The key terms/concepts are the basis for individual lessons. Very often the concept will determine how much time is necessary for student understanding and what instructional strategies are employed to teach it.

LESSON PLAN

Although many models exist for lesson planning the authors find this method useful. It includes all the elements of a well-organized plan. The following example is a good introductory activity.

Objective.   Students will generate a list of problems that would ensue if electricity was indefinitely shut off and a list of possible solutions to those problems.

Procedure.   Teacher begins class with a question after turning off the lights. What would happen if electricity was turned off indefinitely?

The teacher organizes four to six cooperative groups (4–6 students each) and divides the class in half. Half will brainstorm and generate a list of worst-case scenarios in the event of a sustained power disruption. The other half will generate a list of possible alternative sources of energy and how they would be implemented.

Each group will be assigned a spokesperson, who will report the group's responses at the conclusion of the class.

Materials.   Paper, pencil, chalkboard.

Evaluation.   Because this is an introductory activity, an informal evaluation can be done by the teacher. The list generated by each group will give the teacher enough information for an initial assessment. At the conclusion of the "Oil" activity, a formal assessment can be implemented to determine student understanding.

RIVERS

"All places on the Earth have advantages and disadvantages for human settlement. High population densities have developed on flood plains, for example, where people could take advantage of fertile soils, water resources, and opportunities for river transportation. By comparison, population densities are usually low in deserts. Yet, flood plains are periodically subjected to severe damage, and some desert areas such as Israel have been modified to support large population concentrations" (*Guidelines for Geographic Education*, 1984, p. 5).

The subject of this activity chapter is to present the theme, the relationship between human activity and the environment in three different directions: (1) the Nile River, one of the world's greatest river civilizations; (2) the Piscataqua River basin, a New England river, as a model for developing a local river unit; and (3) the future of rivers: scientific and public policy concerns. People continually adjust to adapt to their natural setting in ways that reflect their "cultural values, economic and political circumstances, and technological abilities" (*Guidelines for Geographic Education*, 1984, p. 5). An in-depth study of river settlements and their ecosystems afford teachers opportunities to teach geographical concepts that link history with present and future scientific questions. To investigate a local river in a tangible way allows students to bridge newly acquired knowledge into understanding abstract concepts. When students can understand a local river, they are better able to draw a relation to the world's great river systems and the cultures that sprung from their banks.

Rivers have influenced the development of human activity since the dawn of the distant past. They have provided transportation routes, water for irrigation and drinking, and carried soil that the fertile deltas have fanned from the river's mouth, and in recent times, they have been harnessed to supply electricity to an energy-hungry world. In addition, they have served as seaports and centers of commercial activity, and through the complex network of tributaries have aided in the expansion of economic activity.

The first section, "The Gift of the Nile," provides a historical example of the relationship between the forces of nature and people's ability to adapt and modify them to meet their needs. The second section, "The Great Bay Estuarine System," is a study of the Piscataqua River that separates Maine from New Hampshire. An economic and historical perspective spanning 350 years will provide insights into people's ability to adapt to changing circumstances, thus suggesting a model for students investigating their own local river. The third section, "The Future of Rivers," discusses the implications of the use of rivers today. Technological and public policy questions are presented as problem-solving activities for middle-level students.

The Gift of the Nile

The Nile River, which flows 4,415 miles northward from Equatorial Africa to the Mediterranean Sea, was the source of the greatest of ancient civilizations, Egypt. Human interaction and adaptation to the Nile culminated in the development of agriculture, mathematics, surveying, and religion.

Its predictable ebb and flow created the myth of Isis, goddess of the corn harvest. "In ancient Egypt the reapers were first to lament over the first sheaf cut invoking Isis as the goddess to whom they owed the discovery of corn" (Frazer, 1942, p. 424). As the Nile rose each spring, it brought fertile loess from Central Africa and deposited it on the thin agricultural plain of ancient Egypt, ensuring the annual harvest.

Not only did the Nile carry fertile soil, but it also transported the huge sandstone blocks cut for the three great pyramids at Gizeh and the Step Pyramid at Sakkarak, possibly the oldest structure in the world. For three months of the year preceding the rise of the Nile, 100,000 workers, pressed into service, quarried the stone in the mountains, moved it across the desert, and floated it to its final destination. All of this was done in concert with the predictable rise of the Nile.

Prior to the construction of dikes, canals, and dams to control the annual flooding of the Nile, Egyptians built their homes and villages on mounds. These mounds were built above the high watermark to ensure the safety of the many families who dwelt there. As the people learned to control the river by diverting the water into irrigation ditches and canals to trap water in basins surrounded by dikes, they also learned a major social skill, cooperation. This probably accounts for the reason why the earliest center of community life appeared in Egypt.

A unique combination of the northward flow of the current and the southward breezes aided sailing vessels as they transported products up and down the Nile. The lanteen sail, a triangular sail, could be easily hoisted or lowered, either to be pushed by the wind down the Nile or floated with the current up the Nile. Commerce developed, and the economy expanded as trading flourished.

The ancient Egyptians, wandering nomads from Asia, settled on the banks of the Nile because of the resources the newly discovered natural setting offered. Adapting from hunting and gathering to agriculture, these early colonizers sowed the seeds of a great civilization. As the culture became more complex, division of labor developed. This specialization, which created agricultural surpluses, provided the foundation for the civilization that ultimately developed. Usually, a society that possesses large inventories invites aggression from neighboring groups; however, this did not happen to the Egyptians initially. Natural barriers—to the west, the Sahara, and to the east, another large expanse of arid waste as far as the Red Sea—served as Egypt's major source of protection. The south is yet another barren, waterless wilderness, uninhabited by only a few nomadic Bedouins. The north is protected by many swamps and dangerous waterways, which form the Delta of the Nile. These natural barriers protected the inhabitants of the Nile. Their energies were directed toward building a society, not warring with neighbors.

Paintings on the walls of the tombs of Gizeh and other sites testify to the changes that have taken place between ancient and modern Egypt. These preserved images provide a historical record. From the papyrus swamps, the hippopotamus wallows along with the crocodile. "All over the north the great African fauna withdrew south before the onslaught of aridity; only bones and rock drawings of elephants, rhinoceros, giraffe, and even hippopotamus give evidence of former expanse" (Rzoska, 1978, pp. 23–24). The papyrus swamps have disappeared along with the great mammals.

A subtle shift in climate dramatically affected human possibilities on the Nile. But, as in all human endeavors, people adapted. In Egypt, they exerted greater control on the Nile, bending it to suit their own needs. From the canals and dikes of ancient Egypt to the Aswan Dam of Egypt today, they have both solved and created problems. The need for energy in the industrial world today seems juxtaposed to the quality of the environment. Modern Egypt faces the same conflicts as the rest of the world, defining a balance between people's needs and the ability of the environment to respond.

The Great Bay Estuarine System

The Great Bay Estuarine System, which includes the Piscataqua River as the main drainage river and tidal parts of seven other rivers, separates Maine from New Hampshire, contains over 100 miles of coastline, and is one of the more historically unique regions along the East Coast. This special historical quality is that of a complex maritime region that has invited settlement and development for 350 years.

By their nature, estuaries are natural, aesthetically pleasing places to settle. Their ecological value is in their role as spawning and breeding grounds for fish, as habitats of migratory birds, and as a sponge for floods and filter for river flow.

Three and half centuries of human interaction with this environment have altered but not seriously diminished the ecological balance of the Piscataqua River. (Indian habitation was harmonious with the land and water and the population relatively small, approximately 10,000 in 1600.) Moreover, those centuries have seen the evolution of a regional culture based on some common economic and natural resource needs, as well as increasingly common folklore among those who settled. As much as any other factor, it is the practical know-how and wisdom of those long settled along these rivers and how humans have used and abused them that ties the region together.

The Piscataqua region has undergone considerable and complex change in the last four centuries but has retained some of its original characteristics. To continue to adapt successfully to complex future change, it is necessary to instill historical understanding, including environmental awareness, into the region's population. This is true of all regions throughout the United States contiguous to a river system.

The subdivision of the areas' five original towns of Portsmouth, Kittery, Dover, Exeter, and Hampton produces more than a dozen tidal communities. These towns served as tranship points for inland goods being sent to Portsmouth and, in turn, were recipients of imported products from the main port of Portsmouth. In their own right, the small mills, cottage industries, and other small-scale manufacturers of tidal towns were significant producers for regional export sale. This fluid economy was in full swing by 1750, aided increasingly by the gundalow, originally a floating barge, making Portsmouth one of the major colonial ports. From fishing to boatbuilding and from forestry to mastmaking, one industry spawned another to create a vital regional economy very much a part of expanding world trade. As industry became more complex, the gundalow's design was improved to adapt to the increasing demand for its service. Area towns depended on the gundalow for the transportation of lumber products, agricultural crops, and salt-marsh hay. A feeling of interdependence and community was becoming evident in the region. With this contact came increased river traffic and the exchange of job skills such as boatbuilding and other crafts. Development and its ecological costs surfaced, as forests were denuded and sawdust from mills and other refuse choked the rivers.

Portsmouth's long standing as a major port was dealt a severe blow by embargo, war, and fire in the early 1800s. The regional economy, however, received a major boost from large-scale hydro-powered textile mills, a significant brickmaking industry, and widespread boatbuilding, including the Portsmouth Naval Shipyard. This century saw a much more diverse and complex industrial base to which the gundalow responded by sail, a leeboard, and greater capacity. This larger vessel now carried everything from cotton and textiles to cordwood and bricks, thus becoming a major element in import–export trade.

Such technological development, although an established tradition in the region, served to tighten transportation, and thus communication, more than ever. Business as well as political and social relations were enhanced. A regional consciousness developed among tidal manufacturing towns. The gundalow epitomized this, as the nineteenth century saw the flowering of the vessel as the purveyor of commerce, as well as a unifying force in its port-to-port traveling. As the bearers of news, gossip, and a colorful folklore, gundalow captains and crews had no peers. Dependent on the tides for passage up and down river, and no strangers to mischief and rum, these inland sailors established a rhythm and became a practical and welcomed sight to people in the basin.

As mills moved south and railroad-run national markets left Portsmouth a backwater port, much of the maritime activity at the turn of the century diminished. In contrast, many area towns used shoemaking, leather products, and recreation to keep their economies going, with businesses that were not dependent on the rivers. The demise of the region's maritime life was symbolized by the slow deterioration of the "Fannie M.," the last of the gundalows, at Dover Point in the 1920s. Although the gundalows and the river had given way to motor trucks and paved roads, they had established a sense of place in the Piscataqua region that would live on.

In the twentieth century, the lower Piscataqua River underwent a major industrial transformation, as the Newington–Portsmouth shore became lined with heavy industry, from large-scale fuel storage and a power plant to steel cable production and scrap metal export. Portsmouth's designation as a foreign trade zone will further increase this revitalization and pour new blood into local businesses. Ocean-going traffic is a regular feature in Portsmouth, enhanced by the fishing fleet. The rest of the estuary includes moderate recreation, fishing, and occasional tourist traffic. All this development comes at a price, as several oil spills have marred the estuary, and potential for further pollution and industrial waste problems is present. Population pressures in area towns have put a strain on some land and water resources, so that careful planning and tax reform have become priorities. As the region faces the next century, it must come to grips with its industrial history and decide how much more development the area can absorb before all vestiges of the past are irreparably altered.

The port city of Portsmouth has experienced a historical and cultural renaissance in the past 30 years, spawned by the restoration of Strawberry Banke, a historic waterfront neighborhood. The city continues to fulfill its historic role as the most vital link in the region's maritime heritage and as a focal point for regional cultural and intellectual activities of all kinds.

This analysis explains a variety of changes that the region has experienced over the years. A closer look reveals both subtle and obvious ways in which people of the area have adapted to that change. Farmers who built gundalows during their spare time in the winter made several modifications to the craft to transform it from a crude barge to a major cargo carrier. Local skilled craftspeople modified their skills and learned new ones as changing industries demanded it. Shipyards built dozens of privateers to meet the growing needs of ocean-going trade and fishing fleets. Portsmouth had a serious adjustment to make in its fall from maritime preeminence and its loss of political power to the Merrimack Valley in the nineteenth century. Town centers moved increasingly inland away from the river and landing areas and toward the newly paved roads of the 1920s. In these latter town examples one can see that better use of resources and more foresight would have led to less economic stagnation and a more diversified economic base, but these are some of the lessons of historical change only learned through hindsight. All these changes suggest significant change in water and land use. The lesson of temporarily ignoring waterfront areas has not been lost on many tidal towns that are now viewed as important resources of continuing significance and practical value.

The previous discussion shows how the development of the Piscataqua Basin is a microcosm of the development of the nation—how the social and cultural history is affected by natural resources. Railroads and highways were built, clay was taken from riverbanks for bricks, mills provided new jobs and sometimes polluted rivers, but, overall, the rivers remained constant, unchanging aspects of life in the region. By learning of their past, people may come to appreciate the region more as their own and work to preserve what is worth saving.

The study of the ancient Egyptians' relationship to the Nile River and an overview of 350 years of settlement along the banks of the Piscataqua River provide two examples that can be used as models for the investigation of national, state, and local rivers that have an impact on the lives of students. History and geography become the twin streams that connect the past to the present, disciplines that enable students to recognize their place in time. "To learn geography is to gain in power to perceive the spatial, the natural connections of an ordinary act; to learn history is essentially to gain in power to recognize its human connections" (Dewey, 1902, p. 210). But for middle school students to understand their place in the continuous history of mankind requires starting from the present. "The starting point of history is always some present situation with its problems" (Dewey, 1902, p. 214). An investigation of the current state of rivers and streams will provide students with a basic framework in order to search backward into history for the causes that create the present problems and forward into the future as they propose solutions.

The Future of Rivers

From the East Coast to the West Coast, cities along rivers and harbors are faced with billions of dollars to pay for cleanup efforts as a result of human abuse. "Metropolitan Boston will have to pay $6 billion to bring their harbor in line with the 1972 Clean Water Act requirements. As if that weren't bad enough, they could be coughing up another $2 billion—beyond the Environmental Protection Agency's requirements—to make it safe for fishing and swimming. Along with Boston, several cities on the East and West coasts—San Diego is the other main example—now have to drum up billions of dollars they need to build facilities for secondary treatment" (Harleman, 1990, p. 60).

Since the earliest river settlements, man has created pollution, initially from organic wastes dumped directly into the rivers and salinization of irrigation systems. The severity of the problem increased as populations grew. Today, the technology used to create a better society has indeed been responsible for some of the most critical problems. "There are three major sources of water pollution: domestic waste water, industrial effluents, and land use runoff, although leaching from mine tailings and solid waste dumps and the atmospheric deposition of pollutants into water bodies are of growing importance" (World Resources, 1990–1991, p. 162).

Domestic Waste Water

Large concentrations of population areas that use rivers as its sewer have a severe impact on the life of a river. Domestic waste water is discharged directly into streams, increasing biochemical oxygen demand (BOD). "As it decays, this organic waste depletes the water of oxygen essential to aquatic life and upsets the natural balance of the aquatic ecosystem" (World Resources, 1990–1991, p. 162). If waste water is left untreated, the oxygen level may drop to levels harmful to aquatic life.

Diseases are often carried downstream with untreated sewage. Pathogenic bacteria and viruses derive from human feces. In developing countries, *Salmonella typhosa* has been linked to high infant mortality. Even in developed countries, untreated sewage will present similar problems.

Industrial Effluents

A second problem is the impact of industrial effluents on water quality. Factories and industrial plants along rivers have contributed to reduced water quality and the death of streams as a result of direct dumping of pollutants into the rivers. Textiles, paper, chemical, petrochemical, and food processing industries have dumped their waste into streams and rivers. In addition to direct dumping, combustion of fossil fuels in automobiles and industries that release sulfur and nitrogen compounds into the atmosphere enter bodies of water through acid rain. Areas in the Northeast are increasingly vulnerable to the destruction of lakes and rivers.

Land Use Runoff

The third problem is land use runoff. As people's need for increased agricultural production for food and logging for shelter continues, so do problems associated with land use runoff. Fertilizers and pesticides directly flow into rivers, dramatically affecting water quality. "In the United States, the average monthly salinity level in the San Joaquin River in California increased from approximately 0.28 grams per liter in the late 1930s to 0.45 grams per liter in the mid-1970s. These increases may have harmful effects on downstream agriculture or on areas abutting the rivers" (World Resources, 1991, p. 164). "A five year study (completed in 1980) of more than 150 rivers showed that 42–82 percent of all water sediment samples were contaminated by organochlorine insecticides and 2–7 percent contaminated by organophosphate insecticide" (World Resources, 1990–1991, p. 165).

In addition to the three sources of water pollution—domestic waste water, industrial effluents, and land use runoff—other factors also contribute to the destruction of aquatic ecosystems. If water is drawn from rivers to support irrigation and is not replenished, it will ultimately affect the quality of water downstream. This water is often polluted chemically, biologically, and thermally.

The next section provides teachers with critical thinking activities that can be used when teaching about the Nile River, a local river, and human adaptation to rivers in the future. From these modifications and extensions, activities can be developed to reflect the specific abilities of students and availability of community resources.

River Activities

1. Investigate the extent of water pollution in the river closest to your school. How is the river currently being used? What are the effects of that use on the river?
2. Research and write a community history based on a local river from early exploration, settlement, economic changes over time, technological advances, and future predictions. A good class activity!
3. Compare and contrast early civilizations and how their cultures adapted or were influenced by rivers. What specific contributions flowed directly from their adaptation to the river?
4. Research inventions and technological adaptations to meet the demands of rivers over a historical time span. For example, changes in boat designs, mills, irrigation systems, water power, and hydroelectric power.
5. After investigating a local river, create an Egyptian mural depicting life as it is today in your community.
6. Select a major problem that affects your local river and propose recommendations that will help solve it. Think about the costs, who is going to pay for it, and what the ultimate effect will be. As a guideline for determining water quality, use the following Water Quality Objectives (Swinerton, 1973, p. 6)

Objective 1: Suitable for any use. Water quality uniformly excellent.

Objective 2: Suitable for bathing and recreation; irrigation and agricultural use; good fish habitat; good aesthetic value. Acceptable for public water supply with filtration and chemical treatment.

Objective 3: Suitable for recreational boating; irrigation of crops; habitat for wildlife and game fishes acceptable; industrial cooling and most other industrial uses adequate; not used for human consumption unless boiled.

Objective 4: Suitable for recreational boating and fishing in upper sections of river; oxygen level higher during periods of fish migrations; industrial cooling and some other industrial uses.

Objective 5: Suitable for power; navigation; and some industrial uses.

References

Dewey, John. (1902). *The Child and the Curriculum*. Chicago: University of Chicago Press.

Frazer, James George. (1942). *The Golden Bough*. New York: Macmillan.

Guidelines for Geographic Education. (1984). Association of American Geographers and National Council for Geographic Education.

Harleman, Donald F. (1990, April). "Cutting the Waste in Waste Water Clean Ups." *Technology Review.* In *Annual Editions Environment 91/92.* Guilford, CT: Duskin Publishing Group.

Rzoska, Julian. (1978). *On the Nature of Rivers: With Case Stories of Nile, Zaire, and Amazon.* The Hague and Boston: Dr. W. Junk.

Swinerton, E. Nelson. (1973). *The Dead River.* Athens, OH: Union Printing Co.

World Resources. (1990–1991). *A Guide to the Global Environment.* New York: Oxford University Press.

OIL: IMPLICATIONS FOR
GLOBAL INTERDEPENDENCE

Since the discovery of oil in 1859 by Edwin Drake in Titusville, Pennsylvania, the industrial world has become dependent on it. Industrial nations have built their entire social structure and economic systems on the assumption that oil would be forever forthcoming. As countries discovered oil reserves in the Middle East, their relations with foreign governments became more complex. The international structure of world order and particularly of regional stability has resulted from alliances forged from the need for oil. In recent times, governments have formed alliances based on producing nations and nonproducing nations in an attempt to control both the supply and price of oil. As we look toward the twenty-first century, students need to become aware of the complex issues associated with one of our basic energy resources.

Movement, the fifth geography theme suggested in *Guidelines for Geographic Education* (1984), provides the focus for the activity on oil. Movement demonstrates interdependence and involves people, ideas, and products. Because of oil's international implications, this section will discuss essential elements of global geography. As Alan Backler has written, "global geography provides young people with perspectives, information, concepts and skills essential to understanding themselves, their relationship to the earth, and their interdependence with other people of the world . . . [and] reinforces and extends the process of critical thinking and problem solving . . . applicable to all parts of the curriculum" (Backler, 1988, p. 4).

"Today, nearly two-fifths of the oil consumed by the free world's economy is vulnerable to terrorism, accident, warfare, and extortion. The sudden loss of Persian Gulf oil for a year could stagger the world's economy, disrupt it, devastate it, like no other event since the Great Depression of the 1930s" (Nye, 1991). During the 1970s, oil disruptions were viewed only as an energy issue by most observers. Few realized the ominous threat to world economic security that the oil problem posed. In the United States, until the Airborne Warning and Control System (AWAC) debate in Congress there had been little or no public debate on issues linked to the Persian Gulf that clearly affect the well-being of a democratic society.

The United States' dependence on oil, as well as most other industrial nations', including Western Europe and such Pacific neighbors as Japan, will continue to influence international relations. It is the intent of this activity to provide teachers with the following, so that they can supplement their lessons on energy resources, particularly oil, in a global context:

1. An overview of the world's major oil reserves
2. A history of U.S. involvement in the Middle East since the 1956 Suez crisis
3. The conflict between two dominant value systems: modernization (the West) and tradition (Islam)
4. Critical thinking activities based on changing geopolitical and economic conditions

The World's Major Oil Reserves

Oil is one of the world's nonrenewable resources. A nonrenewable resource exists in limited amounts, and once it has been used it is gone forever. Because it is a fossil fuel like coal and natural gas, it was formed millions of years ago by plants and animals. Countries continue to search for new oil reserves, as it is an irreplaceable resource. Recent discoveries have taken place in the North Sea and Alaska's North Slope.

Oil reserves are located throughout the world and in some of the most unlikely places, from the frozen Arctic wastelands to the scorching deserts of the Middle East. The countries with the largest known deposits of oil include Saudi Arabia, Iran, Kuwait, the nations of the former Soviet Union, Canada, Mexico, and the United States. Although oil deposits are located in other areas of the world, such as under the major oceans, they probably will not be extracted until a cost-effective technology is developed.

During the early half of the twentieth century, the United States was essentially oil self-sufficient. Oil from the Southwest and from wells off the Louisiana coastline produced inexpensive energy. A marriage between oil producers and the automobile industry ensued as a result of low-cost energy. Our industries flourished and the economy expanded, fueled by what appeared to be an unlimited supply. However, two major forces changed this situation: consumption and depletion. The more we consumed, the less we had.

In order to sustain our economy and lifestyle we had to explore for other sources of oil. The Middle East was the most obvious direction, because oil reserves were plentiful and oil was inexpensive to produce. A study in 1960 declared that the average cost of production in the Middle East was $0.16 per barrel, compared with $1.73 in the United States (Heilbroner & Thurow, 1981). Once the United States decided to import oil from the Middle East, it became involved in a complex web of international relations, abrupt price hikes, regional conflicts, and greater national insecurity as it became heavily dependent on oil. The next section provides an analysis of the United States's involvement in the Middle East since the 1956 Suez crisis.

The Suez Crisis of 1956

The study of history is a necessary prerequisite for understanding most current problems. Oil, with its implication for world order and U.S. interests in the Persian Gulf, is no exception. In retrospect, a series of events unfolded, leaving the world with its current oil problem. An analysis of these events will help students gain insight into how oil in the Middle East, regional differences, and international ability are directly linked to our own national security.

The Suez crisis set the stage for our current energy and security problems. Three struggles converged to place in sharp relief the problems and perils the United States would face vis-à-vis its relations in the Persian Gulf region: U.S.–Soviet relations, nationalism versus colonialism, and a threatened NATO alliance. In the summer of 1956, President Abdul Nasser of Egypt nationalized the Suez Canal, violating the International Convention of Constantinople of 1888. He defended his actions in an emotional speech declaring his independence from imperialism, hailing nationalism "as a symbolic act which would set forth Arab Nationalism on its course from the Atlantic to the Persian Gulf" (Stoessinger, 1979). The canal served as a symbol; for Egypt, the growing power of her new nationalism, and for Great Britain, the controller of the canal, her status as an empire. France, already incensed at Egypt for supporting the Algerian revolution, regarded the canal seizure as the last straw.

Great Britain, France, and Israel invaded Egypt, which forced the United States to call for the cessation in the U.N. General Assembly. On the same day, the Soviet Union took up the Egyptian cause and threatened to send aid and bomb London and Paris. The United States confronted its first of many dilemmas. Its actions created severe strains with its allies Great Britain and France and, at the same time, appeared to favor Soviet policy. Nasser, although suffering a military defeat, gained a major political victory. The United States supported Arab nationalism.

When the crisis was over, three changes emerged. First, in terms of the U.S.–Soviet struggle, the Soviet Union had come off best. As Stoessinger (1979) states, "The promulgation by the United States of the Eisenhower Doctrine in March 1957 pledging American assistance to Middle Eastern countries against Communism was testimony to the increasing awareness of this latest Soviet gain" (p. 58). Second, nationalism bested colonialism as Nasser gained political victory. Third, relations between Britain, France, and the United States seriously endangered NATO. Ten years later, another dispute occurred in the region, creating another dilemma for the United States. Israel attacked Egypt, Jordan, and Syria.

The 1967 Arab–Israeli War

"Few issues have been considered more critical to American foreign policy makers than the Arab-Israeli dispute" (Quandt, 1977, p. 1). The 1967 war was a natural consequence of the 1956 Suez crisis. Although the principal actors were the same, the basic issues, "the specific alignment of forces were quite different" (Stoessinger, 1979, p. 159). On May 18, 1967, Secretary U Thant withdrew the U.N. Emergency Force from the Sinai, Gaza Strip, and Sharm El-Sheik at the request of President Nasser. Israel, Syria, and Jordan mobilized their forces on their respective borders. On May 20, the Arab League issued a joint declaration stating an attack on one would be an attack on all.

In addition, Nasser blocked the Gulf of Aqaba, cutting off Israeli's only southern port at Elath. Israel's response was predictable. As an act of war, she would take appropriate action. U.S. President Johnson described the blockade as "illegal and potentially disastrous to the cause of peace" and supported the settlement reached at the conclusion of the 1956 crisis. This time, the United States supported Israel. However, the Soviet Union blamed the Israelis for increasing tensions in the Middle East. In addition, the Soviets supported Arab nationalism against the powers of colonialism.

The situation deteriorated until June 5, 1976, when Israel launched a successful 6-day war against Egypt, Jordan, and Syria. Israel captured the Sinai and the Gaza Strip and destroyed Soviet-supplied hardware.

What were the specific outcomes of the conflict? First, the Soviet Union ended up supporting a loser with the additional burden of having to supply dependent Arab states. Second, superficially, the United States supported a winner. Third, Britain and France maintained distance and, thus, were only marginally affected. Fourth, Israel did not withdraw her forces as she had done in 1956; therefore, the conflict that led to the 1967 war was not resolved. "The United States found itself supporting Israel's hold on newly conquered territories pending Arab willingness to make peace. It would not be long before the dilemmas of such a policy would become evident" (Quandt, 1977, p. 71). Following on the heels of political instability in the Middle East another problem emerged. The oil-producing nations raised the price of oil dramatically.

The 1970 Oil Price Increase

As a result of the rocketing price hikes of oil and their relationship to the economies of Western Nations, the Church Subcommittee Report on Oil (1975) issued the following warning:

> The United States and the rest of the non-Communist world face a most serious economic crisis since the depression of the Nineteen Thirties. If strong policies are not immediately adopted, this crisis can undermine the economic foundation of the non-Communist world and jeopardize our democratic form of government. While the present international economic crisis is complex, its principal cause has been the revolutionary rise in crude oil prices (pp. 8-378–387).

In 1974, oil-consuming nations realized an $80 billion increase in their oil import bill, which led to an unprecedented transfer of the world's wealth. The report cited that the current account surplus of the OPEC countries was $65 billion and that if the trend continued the surplus would be as high as $600 billion by the end of the decade.

The United States' response to the crisis was based on three assumptions: (1) market forces would lead to a drop in the price of crude oil; (2) the United States would develop a special relationship with the government of Saudi Arabia, which in turn would bring about lower international oil prices; and (3) the massive financial flows to the producer nations could be recycled through the existing private banking structure, particularly the Euro-currency market. These assumptions turned out to be mistaken. Prices continued to be set by OPEC rather than by supply and demand, the Saudis were more interested in maintaining relations with the Arab world than pleasing the United States, and private banks were incapable of recycling oil-producer deposits to deficit oil-importing countries.

This problem created both domestic and foreign policy problems for the U.S. government. Domestically, inflation during this period rose to 18%, and correspondingly, interest rates hit a historic high of 22%. Oil consumers found themselves waiting hours in gasoline lines, and home heating bills skyrocketed. Unemployment rose, as heavy energy users adjusted to the sudden price shocks. Internationally, the United States found itself competing for oil against its allies.

The fuel shortages in the United States in the winter of 1973–1974 were a result not only of the Arab oil embargo but, more important, of the failure of the U.S. government to anticipate and devise an effective strategy for coping with the developing strength of OPEC well before the October war of 1973. In 1974, the Secretary of State, Kissinger, and the Secretary of the Treasury, Simon, devised a two-pronged policy: (1) the development of conservation goals (reduction in current oil consumption of 3 million barrels a day by the end of 1975); and (2) a financial safety net of $25 billion worth of loans for industrialized countries each year in 1975 and 1976.

What Happens When Oil Supplies Are Disrupted?

Any number of events can disrupt the flow of oil from the Middle East. When that happens, the threat of inflation is imminent, followed by a serious recession. Immediate results are gasoline lines and the fear of heating oil shortages. When disruptions have occurred in the past, the United States was unable to cope with the crisis. "Both times domestic allocation programs designed to minimize dislocations made the problem worse. Both times, the improvised machinery to deal with the interruption proved to be woefully inadequate" (Alm, Colglazier, & Kates-Garnick, 1981, p. 303).

Even a small loss of production or disruption can set in motion potentially damaging results. Between November 1978 and March 1979, Iranian oil production fell 3.8 million barrels a day. Production outside Iran rose 1.8 million barrels per day but was not enough to offset the difference. This resulted in a reduction of 4% of the free world's oil production. Three problems occur when supplies are reduced: (1) direct disruption of supply, (2) economic damage, and (3) weakening of American foreign policy.

In 1979, when the Iranian cutbacks were felt, substantial disruptions occurred in gasoline and diesel fuel in the United States. Diesel fuel and heating oil were at dangerously low levels. Farmers complained to the government in the spring that they would not be able to plant crops because of an insufficient supply of diesel fuel for their farm machinery. The Department of Energy (DOE) increased fuel allocation to farmers to avert the impending agricultural disaster but reduced fuel to truckers. Truckers rebelled, and incidents of sporadic violence occurred until the situation eventually stabilized.

Gasoline shortages brought the crisis home to most Americans. The reasons for this problem were threefold: (1) higher demand, (2) government priorities in allocation of fuel oil, and (3) private stockpile policies. No provisions were made to combat this disruption other than voluntary conservation.

The second problem, economic damage, was felt as world consumers of oil scrambled for much-needed supplies. "The Japanese, many of whose contracts with major oil companies were canceled, set about bidding stockpiles to ninety days supply, almost without regard to cost" (Alm et al., 1981, p. 309). Prices increased by 120% or from $13 per barrel in January to $28 per barrel in December. The economic consequences throughout the world were severe. In the United States, it cost $35 billion more in 1980 to import oil than in 1978. Equally important, the inflation from oil price increases has greatly increased the difficulties of managing the economy, intensifying the 1980 recession.

Third, the Iranian production reduction affected relations between Europe, Japan, and the United States. Instead of engaging in cooperative action similar to that of OPEC, increased competition for oil ensued. Governments were faced with attempting to satisfy international demands while at the same time cognizant of domestic strains brought on by a limited supply of oil.

The Japanese, threatened with contract termination, bidded up prices on the spot market, thus ensuring their own supply while forcing prices up. OPEC was able to continue the upward price spiral to all of its customers. Faced with lower supplies for the upcoming winter, the president of the United States authorized a $5 per barrel subsidy on imported distillate fuel oil. This action angered the allies who already felt the United States was overconsuming and had not enacted conservation measures. Due to the global response to the Iranian cutback and the actions of many governments, international relations became strained, and the United States' ability to conduct foreign policy weakened. A decade later, the United States found itself again faced with another oil-related problem.

Desert Storm 1990

"For the second time within four years the United States has felt compelled to send military forces to the Persian Gulf to protect its vital interest" (Sterner, 1990, p. 39). On August 2, 1990, Saddam Hussein invaded the small oil-rich country of Kuwait, setting off the largest American show of force since the Vietnam War. Four hundred thousand troops were sent to Saudi Arabia, aircraft carriers streamed into the Persian Gulf, and a nervous world waited through the fall of 1990 to see if the United States and its 26 allies would continue the economic embargo already imposed on Saddam or go to war against him. The U.S. Congress and the public were evenly divided on the solution to this issue. To what extent were American interests at stake in the Persian Gulf? How important is Persian Gulf oil to the United States? "If Kuwait exported broccoli, we wouldn't be there now," read a placard at the time (Nye, 1991).

Although there is disagreement as to the precise degree to which oil served as a catalyst for mobilizing an international effort to eject Hussein from Kuwait, it certainly was one of the principle factors (Layne, 1991; Nye, 1991; Quandt, 1990–1991; Rodman, 1991; Sterner, 1990). Other factors were also responsible for the invasion of Kuwait. "The apparently frozen landscape of the Middle East—no progress toward Arab–Israeli peace, no economic success stories, no impressive strides toward democraticization, no new and inspiring leaders—may have given a false illusion of stability; in fact it merely masked political currents with explosive potential" (Quandt,

1990–1991, p. 49). The invasion of Kuwait is directly related to unresolved oil issues in the Middle East. During the Iran–Iraq War, Saddam Hussein was able to pursue a "guns and butter" policy thanks to subsidies from Persian Gulf states (i.e., oil) and credits from the West. In 1989, at the end of the war, Saddam could no longer extort high profits from his neighbors, "and the price of its only export, oil, was comparatively low, partly due to high levels of production elsewhere in the Gulf" (Quandt, 1990–1991, p. 52).

Fearing the consequences of a major economic crisis at home, Saddam demanded concessions from his Gulf neighbors. These were as follows:

1. For Saudi Arabia and Kuwait to write off the billions of dollars of loans from his war with Iran
2. For Kuwait to provide $10 billion in direct aid
3. For OPEC to push the price of oil to $25 per barrel
4. For Kuwait to yield two islands that control Iraq's port at Um Qasr

All of these demands reflected the economic and political implications of Persian Gulf oil. He was unable to achieve his objectives, and on August 2, 1990, the Iraqui army invaded Kuwait.

Why did the United States seize this opportunity to send troops 6,000 miles away—when allies more heavily dependent on Gulf oil responded with less enthusiasm? "The simple answer is that even distant disorder has effects that hurt, influence, or disturb the majority of people living within the United States" (Nye, 1991, p. 56). The Gulf crisis clearly demonstrates how interdependent the United States is with the rest of the world. Oil provides about 40% of America's energy, and 45% of that oil is imported. Roughly one-quarter of that amount comes from the Gulf. "So America's direct energy dependence on the Gulf is less than five percent" (Nye, 1991, p. 56).

Though 5% at first appears inconsequential, this figure fails to take into account the effect of global interdependence. As long as the world depends on one-third of its oil from the Persian Gulf, any disruption or shortfall will have dramatic effects. If price bidding occurs as it has in the past, even the United States will pay more for oil. Two effects are felt when prices are increased: "a larger import bill (economists call this a change in terms of trade), and shocks to the economy that interrupt growth (economists call these macro-economic effects)" (Nye, 1991, p. 57). It seems clear from the analysis presented that the security of the United States is linked to the policies and actions of individuals and countries in the Persian Gulf region. To what extent we as a nation choose to be dependent on Gulf oil will be determined by future domestic energy policy. The following activities are designed to help students understand the complexity of energy issues and how any fluctuation in the supply of oil will affect them.

Strategic Straits: Problem-Solving Activities

1. Discuss the impact a disruption of the Suez Canal traffic would have on Western Europe.
2. What is the environmental impact of oil spills in the world? Think about closed ecological areas, such as the Persian Gulf, and open areas, such as the coastline of Alaska.
3. What might happen is Saudi Arabia decides to cut back on the production of oil in order to avoid an unwanted inflow of unspendable foreign exchange?
4. Japan depends on 90% imported oil to sustain its economy. If a disruption of oil occurred anywhere in the world, what action might Japan take? And how would that affect other countries?
5. Your community and state have been told by the DOE that a reduction in the supply of oil is imminent. As a local representative you have to develop an energy-conservation program to last approximately 6 months. Oil supplies to your area will be cut by 10%. It is October, and winter is coming.
6. Because of the increasing unpredictability of oil supplies and the high cost to explore for new oil reserves, the U.S. government proposes to develop an alternative energy program. This will involve new technologies, giving up things that are familiar, changes in lifestyle, and an overall reeducation in oil consumption. Develop a proposal that would encompass the changes you believe would result and possible ways of solving these new and immediate problems.

Oil: Key Terms and Concepts

Alliance	Inexhaustible resources	Recession
Alternative source	Inflation	Renewable resource
Colonialism	Interdependence	Resource depletion
Conservation	Nationalism	Scarcity
Consumption	NATO	Security
Dependence	Nonrenewable resource	Self-sufficiency
Depletion	OPEC	Supply and demand
Fossil fuel	Opportunity costs	

References

Alm, Alvin E., William E. Colglazier, and Barbara Kates-Garnick. (1981). "Coping with Disruption." In David A. Deese and Joseph S. Nye, eds., *Energy and Security*. Cambridge, MA: Ballinger.

Backler, Alan. (1988). *Church Subcommittee Report on Oil.* (1975).

Guidelines for Geographic Education. (1984). Association of American Geographers and National Council for Geographic Education.

Heilbroner, Robert, and Lester Thurow. (1981). *Five Economic Challenges.* Englewood Cliffs, NJ: Prentice-Hall.

Layne, Christopher. (1991). "Why the Gulf War Was Not in the National Interest." *The Atlantic, 268*(1):55–64.

Nye, Joseph S. (1991). "Why the Gulf War Is in the National Interest." *The Atlantic, 268*(1):54–81.

Quandt, William B. (1977). *Decade of Decisions.* Berkeley: University of California Press.

Quandt, William B. (1990–1991). "The Middle East in 1990." *Foreign Affairs, 70*(1):49–69.

Rodman, Peter W. (1991). "Middle East Diplomacy after the Gulf War." *Foreign Affairs, 70*(2):1–10.

Sterner, Michael. (1990). "Navigating the Gulf." *Foreign Policy, 81*:39–52.

Stoessinger, John G. (1979). *The Might of Nations.* New York: Random House.

WRITE A HISTORY ESSAY

Social studies teachers face two problems in attempting to teach students how to write a history essay: (1) students' reluctance to write about historical events ("Why do we have to write about that? It happened 200 years ago, who cares?"); (2) creating involvement in the process of writing and learning the elements of the craft ("This is s'posed to be taught in Language Arts."). This activity attempts to introduce students to the elements required to write a good history essay. To facilitate the writing process, we present suggestions to create motivation in conducting historical research and strategies for teaching the elements of writing. When students master research and writing skills, they have the tools necessary to develop more sophisticated essays in the future.

The teacher is the editor, and the students are writers. All writers are required to meet deadlines, and students are no exception. Precise time frames can be established by the teacher for each of the areas in the chronology to assist students in completing their essays.

1. Select a topic.
2. Conduct historical research.
3. Write the first draft using the five senses.
4. Critique and rewrite.
5. Write the final copy.

Select a Topic

To create the motivation necessary to ensure that he or she writes the best possible essay, the student needs to feel tied in some way to the event or person. The general topic should include events or individuals indigenous to the local area or region. Let students select their specific topics for investigation. They need to feel invested in the project. At this point, many students will ask for help in selecting a topic. Rather than telling students, create a problematic situation, in an imaginative fashion that the students can identify with, or participate in vicariously. Another possibility is to conduct the "I don't know about . . . event" exercise.

Create a Situation

1. You are a newspaper reporter for the *Granite Monthly* and you are assigned to cover New Hampshire soldiers in Pennsylvania during the Civil War. A skirmish breaks out that leads to the battle of Antietam. Send an eyewitness account to your editor.
2. As Dolly Madison's servant, you write a diary entry the night the British bombarded Washington during the War of 1812. Recount your mistress's actions and bravery.
3. You have just moved to a new city. One rainy day, after unpacking and getting settled, you explore the attic and find a box full of old letters, photographs, and memorabilia. Use the clues in the box to reconstruct the events of which these people were a part and their role in history.

I Don't Know About

Most people know very little about historical events. They may be able to tell you the date the event occurred and a few important people associated with it, but not much more. Ask the class to list all the questions they have or information they don't know about an event or person. Write them on the board. It will be full in a short time. Here is a sample based on the American Revolution:

> I don't know what kind of ships the British sailed.
> I don't know what women did during the Revolution.
> I don't know what Quakers did during the Revolution.
> I don't know how many tea parties occurred.
> I don't know what types of weapons were used.
> I don't know what the causes were.

This board exercise generates a vast number of interesting queries. Collective ignorance is an excellent starting point. No one is threatened, and it is a good way to help students select a topic. Remember, let the student select it. Once it is selected, the next step is to collect historical data.

Conduct Historical Research

A minimum of five sources should be used in the research phase. The intent is to engage students in actual historical research. In addition to the school library, public libraries and historical associations can provide students with ample material and assistance for this activity. However, librarians should be notified in advance of the topic(s) and number of students planning to use the library. In fact, it is a good idea to invite the librarian to class to discuss the available resources and where they are located. Most libraries have a special collections section in which students will need assistance and supervision.

Students should become acquainted with the tools of the historian. The following suggestions will help them wade into historical waters.

1. Students should view and study *artifacts*. These are found in museums, old houses, antiquarian memorabilia, and antique shops.
2. The *written record* (primary source) provides eyewitness accounts of events and transactions. These include old newspapers (microfiche); diaries and journals; ships' logs; church records; provincial, state, and local records; photographs, paintings, and sketches; and letters.
3. Stories told by older family members or senior citizens invited to class promote real excitement and interest. Although the *oral tradition* poses some limitations for students of this age, it provides a real window to the past.
4. Volumes of *secondary sources* fill the libraries. They are excellent for interpretation and general background.

The students' reading ability and level of sophistication need to be determined so the teacher can decide what sources are appropriate, and how they should be introduced. Most of the material can be investigated by students; yet, there are some, such as handwritten records, that the teacher might borrow and show to the class. Discretion is advised for some rare finds.

Students will need 3 × 5 index cards or a loose-leaf notebook to jot notes or quotes. On their cards they will document sources with book and page. For some, it will require a special notebook or box, because the data will need to be organized. Because most libraries now have copy machines, rolls of dimes and quarters are in order if copying replaces note taking.

Once the material has been gathered, now what? Organize it! The standard outline format is all that students need to use. All the information must relate to the topic selected. If it doesn't, throw it away. The student must state the intention, tell the teacher what will be learned, and why it is important. Simply stated—introduction, main body, and conclusion. Each of these categories will be discussed in the critique section. Once the data have been collected and an outline proposed, students write the first draft.

Incorporate the five senses into the essay. If history is to come alive and connect in some way to students, it must be smelled, touched, seen, heard, and tasted.

Write the First Draft Using the Five Senses

Essayists should use five sense descriptions per handwritten page. This will not only create interest for the reader, but it will help students think and feel what it must have been like to live in a different era. In the same way that George Washington never picked up the phone to call Martha, sense descriptions must be easily fit into a historical period.

> *Smell.* The sweet fragrance of apples baking in the kitchen fireplace bubbling and spitting the newly bought cinnamon, blended with the aroma of freshly poured cream.
>
> *Touch.* Rachel spread the down-filled quilt, soft as newly hatched chicks in spring, over her brother's trundle bed.
>
> *Sight.* Sunlight streamed across the freshly mown meadow. The pewter pitcher cast a long shadow from the softly lit taper placed at the end of the well-scrubbed table.
>
> *Sound.* Clanging bells interrupted the termagant squabbling of barn swallows, inviting the congregation to Sunday service. Wagons bumped and clattered over the corduroy road.
>
> *Taste.* Simon savored the vinegar and molasses switchel as he continued to cut hay with his uncle's scythe.

As students use sense descriptions, they will naturally fall into imagery, metaphors, and similes. Once again, the metaphor must fit the situation. "The Mexican landscape was as flat as a tortilla" is better than "the Mexican landscape was as flat as a pancake."

Thomas Wolfe describes autumn in Maine with its frost "sharp and quick as driven nails," its blazing, bitter red maples, and other leaves "yellow like a living light . . . falling about you like small pieces of sun" (Wolfe, 1961, p. 177). Basic elements of good writing should be taught and reinforced, even by social studies teachers. When the "rough" or "working" draft is in process, students will read sections to the class for criticism.

Critique and Rewrite

Students need to learn how to critique the work of others, as well as how to accept criticism. Setting the conditions for this falls to the teacher. The teacher, as editor, shows enthusiasm, discusses a good idea, and then has the student think about a better way of expressing it, at all times using positive reinforcement. The critique should be a positive process aimed at improving the quality of each student's essay. Students who offer comments must be reminded initially to be courteous and sensitive to others' feelings. Students may critique by presenting positive comments first and one helpful suggestion. The forum is a place where students are assisted in generating new ideas, checking for historical accuracy, reconsidering what they have written, and rewriting to improve their essay.

Revision for students is somewhat different from what it would be for a mature writer. The first draft, by definition, is exploratory, omits material, most often does not have a strong introduction or conclusion, but it does provide a structure from which to add, delete, and change the order of information. In some instances, the student may decide to scrap the topic and select a new one. The most difficult task for students is to accept the idea that several revisions may not only be necessary but are fundamental to good writing. Bruce Catton, the highly successful Civil War historian, admits to constant revision of his work. Class time and homework time should be set aside for student revision with specific assignments. For instance, rewrite using active voice only, check for historical accuracy, or take what you have written and cut the number of words in half. It works, but be prepared for a maelstrom on your first attempt. At least three formal teaching periods should be devoted to the introduction, main body, and conclusion. Other periods can be used for peer review in small groups, individual writing, and general discussion.

A good introduction grabs the reader immediately. Getting students to write and present orally "grabbers" and "gotcha" sentences is time well spent. Almost any American will tell you that the American Revolution started in Lexington and Concord with the shot heard round the world, yet the fact is that the first hostilities against the Crown took place at Fort William and Mary in New Castle, New Hampshire, on December 13 and 14, 1774, after Paul Revere rode to Portsmouth, New Hampshire, to warn the Committee of Safety of General Gage's intentions.

Unknown facts, twists of fate, ironies, and unusual situations constantly turn up in students' research. Use them to help students develop a "grabber." John Paul Jones was a cabin boy at the age of 12 and commanded his first ship at age 16. The average woman spinning wool walked 20 miles a day in front of the spinning wheel. "Grabbers" are developed from facts such as these.

Once the introduction is written and has captured the reader's attention, the writer must continue to hook or pull the reader along by a series of well-developed paragraphs. This section is the main body. Each subtopic heading from the outline is a new paragraph or aspect that further develops the central idea or thesis. Several related facts support each new idea. An essay can be conceived like a mobile, geometric and balanced.

Main Idea
"Grabber"

Subtopic   Subtopic   Subtopic
Fact   Fact   Fact   Fact   Fact   Fact   Fact   Fact   Fact

Conclusion

Which subtopic comes first? That depends on how the writer chooses to present the material. Historical events develop chronologically, year by year, or as a series of incidents leading to an outcome followed by consequences. In the case of a historical figure, one can begin at birth and recount significant experiences culminating in the action(s) that made the person famous. "The chronological method is almost always the best way to write history or biography and is almost essential for explaining a process in which time relationships play an important role" (Bates, 1978, p. 67).

The most difficult paragraph for students to write is the conclusion. Some writers argue that the conclusion should come no later than the second paragraph of the essay itself, others at the end. What does a middle schooler do? Develop a sentence that draws a relationship between the central idea of the essay and a modern problem or consequence: *As a result of the terrible losses suffered at Pearl Harbor, the United States today spends billions of dollars on national defense.* Showing a relationship between the past and the present helps students understand that the present is an extension of the past and that events do not take place in a vacuum. But more important, the students have drawn the relationship. In a sense, they are historians.

References

Bates, Jefferson D. (1978). *Writing with Precision*. Washington, DC: Acropolis Books Ltd.

Wolfe, Thomas. (1961). "No Door." In Hugh C. Holman, ed., *The Short Novels of Thomas Wolfe*. New York: Charles Scribner's Sons.

INTEGRATING SOCIAL STUDIES AND LITERATURE

The history of a people—its culture, mores, and religions—is transmitted through literature. Children at very early ages are told and read fairy tales, folk tales, Bible stories, and myths as part of cultural socialization. In the same way *Grimm's Fairy Tales, Aesop's Fables,* and religious parables encompass universal traits; Paul Bunyan, John Henry, Johnny Appleseed, and George Washington and the cherry tree suggest individual traits peculiar to the American character. Therefore, the study of literature and social studies should not be viewed as separate entities but, rather, as a single whole.

Thus, social studies and literature should be taught together. Bruno Bettelheim (1977) stated that the most important and most difficult task in raising a child is to help him or her find meaning in life. "To find meaning one must be able to transcend the narrow confines of a self-centered existence and believe that one will make a significant contribution to life" (p. 1). The two experiences necessary to promote a child's ability to find meaning are: (1) parental love, and (2) transmission of one's cultural heritage. Literature is the best vehicle to achieve the second.

Literature can sow the seeds for both intellectual and emotional development. Stories provide the flint that sparks the imagination and allows the child to derive a wealth of meaning from activities. "Geography is a topic that originally appeals to the imagination—even to the romantic imagination" (Dewey, 1916). A child's interest is piqued when adventure, travel, and exploration are presented through literature.

Literature is a broad term and needs to be further examined. Although it typically falls into three subdivisions—fiction, nonfiction, and poetry—it can also be divided further into the following discrete subgroups: poetry, folk tales, fairy tales, myths, legends, fables, fantasy, historical stories, realistic stories, and informational literature (Georgiou, 1969).

Integrating Social Studies and Literature

What genres lend themselves to teaching social studies, and how they might be introduced to middle school students is the focus of this next section. The folk tales and fairy tales are examples of the oral tradition. They are usually fast-moving stories of adventure, comedy, or romance, but of interest to social studies is the fact that the plot, character, language, and mannerisms of the personalities mirror the respective culture.

Myths, fables, and legends come to us from the distant past. They were ancient man's attempt to explain the forces of nature or to perpetuate the deeds of gods and heroic men. "Civilizations derive their life force from man's endless pursuits of knowledge about himself, the world in which he lives, and his relationships to this world" (Georgiou, 1969, p. 216). Teaching myths in social studies classes affords students the opportunity to gain historical insights into the values of past cultures.

Historical and realistic stories appeal to the vicarious nature in all of us and, at the same time, provide specific examples of how characters lived in their actual setting. *The Adventures of Tom Sawyer, The Adventures of Huckleberry Finn*, and *Little House in the Big Woods* offer students the opportunity to learn what life was like in pioneer days. All types of literature, however presented, offer teachers a variety of ways to teach social studies and literature simultaneously. Several examples will not only demonstrate how this goal can be achieved, but also, more important, will give teachers ideas they can use when designing their own curriculum.

Fairy tales are extremely effective when told or read to elementary students and are just as valuable to middle school students. However, older students don't want to be assigned "little kids'" stories. The methods employed need to change. During the sixth grade many students study culture and civilizations; therefore, create activities in which students are archaeologists or anthropologists. One of the artifacts they need to examine in attempting to understand a particular culture is a copy of a myth or fairy tale. How are the values of that culture expressed through the piece of literature? The tale will not only reveal cultural foundations, but it will also allow students an opportunity to confront those inner forces that help a young person to find meaning in life.

Typical of most state curriculum guides, the State of Wisconsin's *Guide to Curriculum Planning in Social Studies* (1986) recommends that the following topics be investigated at the sixth-grade level. "What major civilizations have thrived in the past and what have they contributed to world history? and how do geographic and environmental forces influence the distribution and concentration of world population?" (p. 62). It seems to us a perfect chance to integrate social studies concepts and literature.

The setting of a story provides an avenue to discuss the environment, which includes physical geography and climate. Characters always have names and occupations indigenous to a historical cultural setting. In the case of fairy tales, for instance, the antagonist is a tsar, feudal baron, sheriff, or witch. In addition to the issue of good versus evil, as exemplified by the characters, political authority, power relationships, and basic forms of government can be explored. Character placement and treatment in the family often provide clues in understanding family and social life.

Two Russian fairy tales, "Nianya's Little Pigeons" and "The Sweet-Stringed Dulcimer" (Carpenter, 1933), provide excellent examples of how social studies concepts fly from the pages like the spray of snow from a fast-moving troika gliding across the Russian steppe. Almost all fairy tales evolve from a specific cultural context. The history, geography, and economic conditions have been woven into the basic fabric of the tale so much so that social studies concepts are inescapable elements of a story.

The following excerpt is taken from "Nianya's Little Pigeons" to demonstrate the importance of social studies concepts as they relate to a complete understanding of the story for the reader.

"Nianya's Little Pigeons"

For several days the white snowflakes had been falling, falling. The great Russian country house had been hidden away from the outside world by swirling veils of white. From the playroom, Kyril and his sister Sonia could not even see the tall birch tree at the corner of the house, so thick were the flying flakes.

Now at last the snow ceased. The Russian countryside lay under a blanket of white. The branches of the trees were bent beneath their loads of clinging snow, and the outbuildings and peasant's huts above the great courtyard behind the house were almost smothered in white drifts.

Winters are cold in the land where Kyril and Sonia live. And the cold weather means big appetites. In the home of the poor peasant, the hungry children had to fill their stomachs from the great bowl of cabbage soup, set out for each meal on their rude table, with chunks of black bread made from the rye grown by their father. But in a rich country house like that of Kyril and Sonia, the fare was much better.

In just these few passages, the concept of climate is suggested by the amount of snow, latitude by the birch tree, social conditions by contrasting the peasants' huts with the rich country house, and food with the introduction of cabbage soup and rye bread. A second tale will exemplify additional social studies concepts.

"The Sweet-Stringed Dulcimer"

Far, far away, beyond the blue sea, in a vast kingdom, there reigned a Tsar and the Tsarina, his wife.

To the delight of the Tsar and Tsarina there were born to them two little daughters, Princess Priceless and the Princess Invaluable.

* * *

At last Fedor arrived at a thick forest. He stopped to listen, for some strange noises came out of the wood. On he went among the trees, with fear in his heart. And what did he see? Two forest giants were fighting and fighting. One hit the other with a great oak tree, and the other struck back with a tall pine. Fedor began to play music upon his sweet-stringed dulcimer. The forest giants ceased their battle and began to dance and to sing. At last, worn out, they fell down upon the green earth.

Tsar and *tsarina*, along with the two princesses, introduce the concept of royalty, which allows the teacher to explore with students the relationships between peasants and kings and queens. Once again, in this tale, oak trees and pines give a sense of geographic location.

Moving from the fanciful toward the historical is yet another way middle-level students can benefit from the integration of social studies and literature. "Fine historical stories invite readers to live an adventure in the past vicariously. Young readers can thus witness historical events, meet historical characters, recapture the flavor of an era, and enter a new world whose experiences can deepen and broaden" (Georgiou, 1969, p. 304). In that process students begin to view themselves as connected to past events and, also, in their newly realized state, perhaps see themselves as making a contribution to the future. Life is a continuous flow, from generation to generation, and through literature, students can begin to perceive themselves as being a part of the great sweep of human destiny.

The activities that can be developed by fusing social studies and literature are as vast as one's imagination. We present several possibilities in the following section. Most literary forms contain four basic elements: plot, character, setting, and theme. In order to understand a piece of literature, these four elements need to be understood. If one uses these elements with the five basic social studies themes, a teacher not only can provide a basic understanding, but also, more important, he or she can provide students with the richness and complexity of most problems. The opportunities to develop complex thinking activities are immense. This method allows students to become more aware of the psychological dimension that Bettelheim feels is necessary and, at the same time, helps create an awareness of the world around them. Table 6-1 enables teachers to ask specific questions and develop additional activities to achieve these goals.

Three model activities—a poem, Carl Sandburg's "Improved Farm Land"; a play, Arthur Miller's *The Crucible*; and a short story, José Vasconcelo's "The Boar Hunt"—illustrate how a teacher can integrate literature and social studies.

Carl Sandburg's poem "Improved Farm Land" describes changes that took place to a piece of land as a result of human endeavors. A felled forest to a standing cornfield reflects the transformation and raises provocative questions. Although people–environment interaction is the focus of Sandburg's imagery, the four other themes will also generate questions.

"Improved Farm Land"[1]

Tall timber stood here once, here on a corn belt farm along the Monon
Here the roots of a half mile of trees dug their runners deep in the loam
    for a grip and hold against winter storms.

---

[1]"Improved Farm Land" from *Slabs of the Sunburnt West* by Carl Sandburg, copyright 1920 by Harcourt Brace & Company and renewed 1950 by Carl Sandburg, reprinted by permission of the publisher.

Then the axmen came and the chips flew to the zing of steel and
   handle— the lank railsplitters cut the big ones first, the beeches
   and the oaks, then the brush.
Dynamite, wagons and horses took the stumps—the plows sunk
   their teeth in—now it is first class corn land—improved
   property—and the hogs grunt of the fodder crops.
It would come hard now for this half mile of improved farm land
   along the Monon corn belt, on a piece of Grand Prairie, to
   remember once it had a great singing family of trees.

Location. Along the Monon railroad, a rail line running north–south in
western Indiana. To what extent did the railroad affect the development
of the Midwest? Of the country?

Place. Western Indiana. What images does the poem provide to help
identify the place? Describe the physical and human characteristics.

Region. Corn belt. Describe the corn belt physically and culturally.

Human–Environment Interaction. Describe the changes that took place and
how they affect both humans and the environment when land is changed
from forest to farmland. How are habitats altered? Is that beneficial? Discuss occupational changes, as well as changes in community life.

Movement. People move from one place to another. Describe the "pull"
factors that brought people into Western Indiana. Where did the people
come from? Why?

The final image, "to remember once it had a great singing family of
trees," offers thoughts for today. Does Sandburg speak to our present generation in "Improved Farm Land"?

The Crucible

A second illustration is Arthur Miller's drama, *The Crucible.* Set in Puritan
New England in 1692, it is a play based on the Salem witchcraft trials. Miller
wrote the play in 1953 to raise social criticism during the infamous McCarthy
era in the United States. He viewed the issues of individual freedom, law and
authority, and social conscience as having a timeless quality.

The Salem tragedy developed from a paradox. It is a paradox in whose
grip we still live, and there is still no promise that we will discover the resolution. Simply it was this: for good purposes, even high purposes, the people
of Salem developed a theocracy, a combination of state and religious power
whose function was to keep the community together and to prevent any kind
of disunity that might open it to destruction by material or ideological purposes. It was forged for a necessary purpose and accomplished that purpose.

However, all organization is and must be grounded on the idea of exclusion and prohibition, just as two objects cannot occupy the same space. Evidently, the time came in New England when the repression of order was heavier than seemed warranted by the dangers against which the order was organized. The witch hunt was a perverse manifestation of the panic that set in among all classes when the balance began to turn toward greater individual freedom (Richards, 1976, p. 12).

A study of the play or a class presentation affords the opportunity to discuss these important ideas and help students understand their responsibility in a democratic society.

Location. Salem, Massachusetts, 1692.

Place. Describe the physical and human characteristics of Salem during 1692. To what extent did severe weather and marauding Indians affect the attitudes of the people?

Region. Northeast or New England. Do particular regional influences affect human behavior? Cite examples from *The Crucible.*

People–Environment Interaction. What impact did clearing land have on the area surrounding Salem?

Movement. What ideological schism developed in Salem that led to the witch hysteria? Describe the characters who contributed to the panic. What were the motives of Tituba? The girls? The faction supporting the fear? How did particular members of the community deal with the accusations? At what point in the play did individual conscience overcome community conformity? What was the result?

An examination of the passions unleashed in 1692 in Salem, Massachusetts, helps analyze the fear and panic that arose in the United States during the anticommunist witch hunts of the 1950s. If history indeed has a timeless quality, it is inevitable that another occurrence will arise at some point in the future. What conditions need to be present for this to happen? What is the responsibility of individuals in our democratic society to prevent this kind of destructive behavior?

Another useful activity is to make a chart either individually or with the class comparing similarities and differences.

1. How is the character the same as or different from you?
2. How is the climate the same as or different from yours?
3. How is the food the same as or different from yours?
4. How are the customs the same as or different from yours?

5. How is the technology the same as or different from that of our country?

This activity allows students to put in relief their own attitudes and values with that of another culture. The purpose of examining another culture or time period is not only to gain an appreciation of that society, but also, more important, to use it as a reference point in reaching an understanding of our own culture.

To conduct the approach that we suggest as a way to integrate social studies concepts with the study of literature (see Table 6-1) requires a variety of types of literature. *Children and Their Literature*, by Constantine Georgiou (1969), is highly recommended; it presents an annotated bibliography of all the major works grouped by age level.

Social studies and literature act in concert in a valuable way for young people. Bettelheim (1977), in explaining the necessity of using fairy tales, says that the message a fairy tale gets across to the child is "that a struggle against severe difficulties in life is unavoidable, is an intrinsic part of human existence—but that if one does not shy away, but steadfastly meets unexpected and often unjust hardship, one masters all obstacles and in the end emerges victorious" (p. 8). The human experience is nothing more than a universal struggle against severe difficulties. Our history is a liturgy of wars, famine, economic failures, and oppression, but it is also a history of progress and promise. Middle-level students need to develop a mechanism for understanding and coping with the realities of the adult world. One way educators can prepare students is to provide a curriculum that satisfies their immediate psychological needs and, at the same time, promotes awareness of the larger world to them.

References

Bettelheim, Bruno. (1977). *The Uses of Enchantment*. New York: Vintage.

Carpenter, Frances. (1933). *Tales of a Russian Grandmother*. New York: Doubleday.

Dewey, John. (1916). *Democracy and Education*. Toronto: Free Press.

Georgiou, Constantine. (1969). *Children and Their Literature*. Englewood Cliffs, NJ: Prentice Hall.

Richards, Stanley. (1976). *America on Stage: Ten Great Plays of American History*. Garden City, NY: Doubleday.

Wisconsin Department of Public Instruction. (1986). *A Guide to Curriculum Planning in Social Studies*. Madison: Wisconsin Department of Public Instruction.

TABLE 6-1   Connecting Social Studies and Literature

	Plot	Character(s)	Setting	Theme
Location	Where does the story take place? Where do things happen?	Where did the characters come from? Where are they going?	Where do the major events take place?	What ideas does the author express about characters and their lives that help us learn some other fact about human nature, our lives, or the lives of others?
Place	What different features allow the action to take place?	Who shows/is aware of physical and cultural characteristics?	How are the special features of "place" described?	
People–environment interaction	How do the characters modify or adapt to their environment?	Who changes the cultural values, economic needs, wants, or abilities?	Where does the natural environment limit/allow the action?	
Movement	What products, ideas, or information move from one place to another?	Who is the mover of the ideas, information, or products?	What comparisons/contrasts are made characters who have been somewhere else?	
Region	How do events define an organized area?	In what ways do the characters show their connections to one another?	What factors determine action, language, religion, government, etc.?	

Source: Adapted from Susan Disbrow, "Connecting Geography and Literature," Wisconsin Geographic Alliance Summer Institute, Madison, WI, 1991.

PRODUCE A NEWS MAGAZINE

Television affects everyone. Many critics point to its negative effects, a decline in reading scores, and the passivity it produces in viewers. Are we becoming a nation of "couch potatoes," victims of the "tube," or can teachers use television as an education tool? A student-produced news magazine turns television from a passive to an active medium.

A well-produced news magazine employs all five themes. World and national maps are used to pinpoint location. Location can also be included with clever leads, such as "U.S. dollar plummets in Tokyo Stock Market" or "High octane fuel spill causes evacuation between Willow Street and Bypass 51." Students want to know where stories took place.

What is the place like? Describe the human and physical characteristics. For example, the howling wind burns the sparse vegetation on the upland plain, pleading for rain. Is this a good place to live? Perhaps it is, but what else do we need to know? One man, John Winter, a third-generation sheep farmer, loves the land and sheep he tends. This proves that even in the most severe climates, humans have found meaning in their lives. Human interest stories come alive when juxtaposed with the environment. Students want to know how other people adapt to their environment and, in the process, how they come to understand their own.

Ever since humans first inhabited the earth, a continual interaction has occurred. Humans have both abused and become stewards of the land. Environmental issues saturate the news. Global warming, acid rain, deforestation, toxic waste, quality of water, and waste management affect everyone. News stories that tell how these issues affect the local community and what needs to be done provide the opportunity to become involved in social action at the local level.

What is moving and why? Weather changes daily as air masses are in constant motion. The weather report helps students follow the movement of storm tracks and high-pressure areas. How will the weather affect us today and tomorrow? A local accident creates a traffic jam and movement stops. How many people are affected and in what ways? Movement takes place in the stock market—up and down. Charts and graphs explain the economy after all the data have been compiled and statistically analyzed. Students can learn to understand the significance of movements by following trends.

Movement occurs when people are affected by drought, fire, flood, volcanoes, and industrial plant closings. Almost every newsworthy event involves movement. One exercise could be to have middle-level students use it to explain the news.

Regional conflict and regional cooperation provide the centerpiece for international news. How does the European Economic Community (EEC)—a good example of regional cooperation—affect exports in the United States and the Pacific Rim nations when a new trade policy has been enacted? The Arab–Israeli conflict and the disintegration of the Soviet Union continue to confound world leaders. As the U.S. economy struggles to recover from the recession of the early 1990s, what will the effect be on the Sun Belt, the Rust Belt, or Silicon Valley? Will regionalism exert an impact on nationalism or globalism as the world strives for a new order? All five themes will aid students in producing an excellent news magazine.

Producing a weekly program affords students the opportunity to learn to write and present ideas concisely, become informed about national and international events, understand weather maps and symbols, and develop interviewing skills. Creativity and imagination bloom when students create sets, make costumes, and dub music to enhance the news show. As a project activity, the news magazine develops interpersonal skills, group work, cooperative learning, and organizational skills, but the real value is that content is not sacrificed.

At a time when the middle school concept is still evolving, the debate between hands-on activities versus content has not been adequately resolved. This activity attempts to achieve a synthesis between the two. For example, students learn content as they prepare their news program. Improvement in skill level is noticeable weekly.

Can 20 to 30 students present the news effectively in a typical 45- to 50-minute period? The next section furnishes a model to achieve that goal, beginning with a well-planned set design and ending with a list of newsworthy items.

The Set

A carefully designed set allows a continuous flow of news. Students need to move freely without knocking over props or disturbing the presenter. Figure 6-1 addresses many problems inherent in a news production.

Three sets, A, B, and C, are designed in the rear of the classroom. Set A is four desks strung together to seat the news team. From this set, national and international news, cooking, and commercials are presented. Behind the news team, a student world map covers the wall. Set B is composed of two chairs flanked by a bookcase and a softly lit lamp. Interviews and book and movie reviews keep the class up to date on what there is to see, hear, and read. Set C, a solitary podium accompanied by a weather map chart, is where the weather, editorials, and sports are presented. In the front of the room, the teacher's desk can be used for audio equipment, producer's signals, and a spotlight that illuminates each set.

For the average middle schooler, moving on and off sets is not as simple as it appears. Students need to know where to go and when, especially when the lights are low. Just before news time, draw the shades. Students should be

WALL

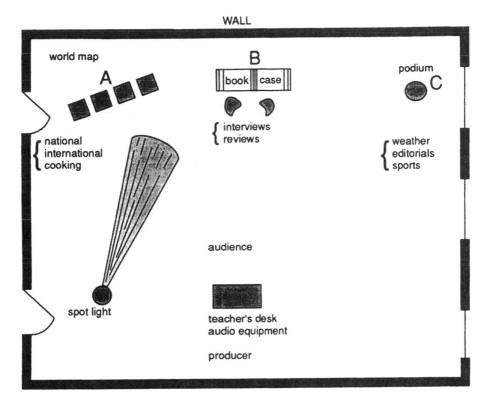

FIGURE 6-1   A News Production Set

in place at sets A, B, and C. At news time, music plays the student theme, the producer introduces the name of the news magazine, and the spotlight flashes on set A, the news team. When national news is complete, the spotlight swings to set B, ready for an interview or book review, as the news team quietly exists set A and is replaced by a second team. The spotlight continues its journey to set C, the weather, and then back to set A.

This model, or a variation of it, creates fluid movements, on and off each set, while the spotlight draws attention to the news of the moment. The producer organizes each segment chronologically, either by number or letter—(1) national news, (2) book review, (3) weather, and so forth—until all students have presented their segments.

News Topics

A student-produced news magazine has the advantage of presenting items of local interest or items that relate to the curriculum. Students will learn that news reporting—who determines what is presented and why—is selective.

For instance, if the class is studying Latin America, shouldn't news from that part of the world be presented in the international report? Natural disasters, such as floods, hurricanes, and earthquakes, might relate to what is taught in science, or a science update segment might be included. Book reviews can include anthologies from language arts or stories related to social studies themes. Through role playing, historical characters can be interviewed; older members of the community with special interests or hobbies that will broaden the curriculum can be guests on the show. Student sports reporters cover their school teams, present the scores, and interview team players. Editorials, allowing students to voice their opinions, provide the forum for responsible discussion, in a point–counterpoint format. With these general thoughts in mind, the following news items will provide ideas that enable students to produce a great news magazine.

Hard News (National and International)
Require students to watch television news and scan local newspapers for hard news. An interesting lead that uses active verbs rivets attention to the story. Facts strung tightly together inform and engage the reader. *Who, what, when, why, where,* and *how,* not necessarily in that order, satisfy the reader's basic curiosity. And a well-conceived conclusion with a memorable fact or image will stay with the reader. Good news stories provide good models for students who are writing their own stories.

Order needs to emerge from chaotic facts and bits of information. An orderly presentation allows students to retain knowledge and, at the same time, develop presentation skills. Two methods work well at the middle school level: (1) the general-to-specific method of development, and (2) the chronological method of development.

The general-to-specific method, or a broad statement followed by a series of specific facts, is easy for most listeners to follow. For instance, "The Defense Department needs to shore up its defenses" might be followed by these statements: (1) "Replacement parts for medium-range bombers are difficult to procure"; (2) "Troop strength in Europe has been cut by 20% to cut costs"; and (3) "Accidents on naval vessels create concern at the Pentagon."

Another system of logical arrangement is the chronological method. According to this method, items or events are ordered in the time sequence in which they occurred. This is particularly useful for news stories. At the national level, the passage of legislation, Supreme Court decisions, and environmental concerns can be reported using the chronological method. World events barrage us nightly, bringing their own history, creating their own dilemmas, and ultimately running their own natural course. As students gain confidence by using these two methods, they will become better informed about events that affect them and also better able to present these events in a logical and coherent manner.

Weather

Everybody talks about the weather. Your students should too. Understanding how weather works, its impact on the personal lives of students, and its effect on the economy are basic areas of learning that this activity addresses. Questions such as "What should I wear today?" or "Why are oranges so expensive?" usually can be answered by a well-prepared weather report.

Cooking

Many students love to cook; therefore, easily prepared dishes can be part of the news magazine. From Julia Child to Jeff Smith, students are familiar with the range of food that can be presented.

Linking food to the curriculum offers an educational device worth exploiting. Indigenous recipes preceded by the history of the dish expand students' awareness of the relationship of food to history and culture. World history courses lend themselves to cooking as a vehicle to explore cultural values, food resources, and the rituals associated with eating. We are what we eat. Why are rice and wheat major staples in some cultures and not in others? Why do some cultures use dairy products, while others do not? How do religious values affect what is eaten and when?

United States history courses can introduce recipes that use corn, beans, squash, and fish to illustrate the early relationship between the colonists and the Indians. "Journey cakes," "Johnny cakes," and "hoe cakes" not only are easy to prepare in class, but also tell something about travel in colonial America. The verse, "Peas, peas, peas, peas, eating goober peas," helps students understand the Civil War.

Some schools do not allow cooking in the classroom; therefore, it may be necessary to improvise. Students can prepare a food update—a "junk food to health food" focus will help students to understand the value of certain types of food. Are fast foods good for you? Culinary sleuths will expose the "fast" foods that slow your body and determine which foods are laced with chemical additives that may prolong their shelf life but not your life. No matter how food is presented, it will leave a lasting taste.

Interviews

People are interesting, and students should have the opportunity to meet them, find out what they do through the news magazine interview, and, in the process, expand their interviewing skills. Local people are often a good source for interesting interviews. They are involved in projects, environmental issues, history, small business, travel, and the professions. Another equally interesting approach is to let students role-play historical characters.

A good interview includes research, well-formulated questions, and conducting the actual interview. Once a speaker or topic has been selected, students conduct research. Depending on the speaker, this might include reading several back issues of the local newspapers, consulting the *Reader's Guide to Periodical Literature* in your library for recent articles, or basic library reference for historical issues. Research information provides the basis for formulating clear, concise questions. Carey and Greenberg (1983) suggest the following guidelines. To conduct the interview I need to

1. Decide on my source; ask the person for an interview; and set a date, time, and place for the meeting.
2. Do background research, so I will be familiar with the material to be discussed and be able to understand the terms used.
3. Make a list of questions I want to ask.
4. Decide if I will use a tape recorder or take notes; make sure my tape recorder is in working order.
5. Practice asking my questions.
6. Review my background notes and questions and delete any questions that are repetitious.
7. Prepare an introduction that will explain to the interviewee the purposes of the interview and how it will be used.
8. Check materials one more time right before the actual interview takes place.

How is the interview going to be presented live on the news magazine? That is up to the individual. The interviewee might consent to a live interview, or students can tape the interview on location and play it on a monitor or report the results of an interview in the body of the news magazine.

Commercials

Follow the principle of "caveat emptor"; that is, let the buyer beware. The adolescent market is targeted by Madison Avenue. Its products for the most part not only promise more than they deliver, but they also "encourage the overconsumption of natural resources and ignore the environmental damage that often goes along with overconsumption" (Weiss, 1980, p. 117). Writing and presenting commercials teaches students to become critical consumers.

Not all advertising is negative. Much of it is useful and necessary for general health and, in many cases, it promotes competition that reduces prices. Students need to know the difference between good and questionable products, so that they can become wise consumers.

Student commercials should include the following elements:

1. *Emotional appeal.* Appeal to patriotism, nostalgia, dogs, small children, and so on. A second category is guilt, shame, anxiety, and fear. Finally, the least commendable appeals are those of ambition, greed, vanity, and self-preservation.

2. *Subconscious.* In the ad game, the appeal to the subconscious is called a "rug" or "carpet." "Scientists know that the subconscious mind takes in far more impressions every second than does the conscious mind. Experiments prove that the human subconscious notices and remembers nearly every detail of every event of a person's life" (Weiss, 1980, p. 52).
3. *Color.* How does red make you feel? Blue? What impressions are created when muted colors are used instead of bold colors? Encourage students to compare colors used for children's medications and adult beverage ads.

Although these suggestions do not cover every area in the gentle art of persuading students to part with their money, they will help students enjoy researching their topics.

Editorial
Students need an avenue to express their concerns on matters that affect them most. The editorial is the forum to discuss and debate the issues they have on their minds. From school lunches to space launches, earthquake victims to endangered species, students want to "speak out."

Before speaking out, students need to ask themselves two questions: "What do I want to say?" and "What is the best way to say it?" People don't remember much. "Herman Ebbinghaus tells us that half an hour after a presentation, the average listener has forgotten 40 percent of what was said. By the end of the day, 60 percent. By the end of the week 90 percent will have been forgotten" (Berg & Gillman, 1989, p. 33). To be heard, students will have to make their point and drive it home.

An editorial urges the audience to show concern and take action. It asks the listener to do something—to vote, to decide, to act. A strong message uses vivid, unambiguous language. Clarity, simplicity, and repetition are the basis for a memorable editorial.

Introduction, main body, and conclusion. What's new? The introduction needs a good lead sentence, or "grabber," to get the audience's attention. "Sixty percent of all middle school students are overweight—what about you?" is better than, "This editorial is going to talk about weight problems among middle school students." Once you have your audience's attention, illustrate the main body with examples, statistics, and anecdotes. Don't tell them, show them. A no-smoking presentation developed the following grabber to dramatize smoking-related deaths. "Almost one thousand people in this country die each day from smoking-related illness. Imagine it. That's as if two fully loaded jumbo jets collided over your hometown everyday—and everyone aboard was killed. We would do something about the air-traffic problem that was responsible. Likewise, we should do something about the smoking problem" (Berg & Gillman, 1989, p. 36). Finally, a well-conceived conclusion should follow. Words grouped in triplets add extra punch to your message and, most important, help the listener remember the message. Bear in mind that the three elements of a good editorial are clarity, simplicity, and repetition.

References

Berg, Karen, and Andrew Gillman. (1989). *Get to the Point*. New York: Bantam Books.

Carey, Helen H., and Judith E. Greenberg. (1983). *How to Use Primary Sources*. New York: F. Watts.

Weiss, Anne. (1980). *The School on Madison Avenue*. New York: Sutton.

GRAVESTONES TEACH LOCAL HISTORY

A field trip to the local cemetery affords students the opportunity to gain insight into local history and provides teachers with an activity that teaches critical thinking skills. A cemetery activity incorporates elements of social studies, art, writing, math, and science. It not only creates interest in those disciplines, but also reinforces basic skills. To middle school students, a visit to the graveyard makes the history of their city or town come alive, both from the form of the carvings and from the events to which the stones bear witness.

Several of the themes create a framework for understanding local history.

Location.   Does the location of a gravestone tell us anything about the deceased person? In the case of Native Americans, does the location of burial mounds reveal anything about their culture? In some cases, unbaptized children were not buried in the cemetery, but outside of it.

Place.   Can inscriptions or artifacts tell students what kind of place the community was? What was the religious background, relative wealth, and ethnic composition of the inhabitants? Early graveyards in New England reveal that there were poor, Protestant and English community members and, in some cases, Native Americans who helped the earliest settlers. As social and technological changes evolved in society, these changes were also manifested in cemeteries. From East to West, American ethnic patterns and values are literally cast in stone.

Movement.   Push–pull factors are easily observed in cemeteries. Burial grounds are a testament to America's pluralism. Throughout the United States, Native American burial grounds exist. It may be interesting to have students compare birth and death dates of persons with their ethnic background. For example, old English grey slate slabs dominate New England cemeteries prior to 1700. In the upper Midwest, Central European and Scandinavian names fill the cemeteries after 1840. The Old South and Southwest reveal the early influence of the French multiethnic society. Why did these populations leave their homelands, and when? Why did they choose to settle in the communities in which they did? Within ethnically diverse communities, each group has its own cemetery. What does this tell us about our country's history? Is this practice continuing today?

In order to begin to answer some of these questions, we suggest the following model: John Dewey's experience-based curriculum (1916) provides the philosophical basis for the activity. Because experience itself is part of the process of adjustment to a changing environment, knowledge is defined in terms of the interaction with a problematic situation. Dewey divides this process into five steps: (1) suggestions leaping forward to a possible solution; (2) the isolation of a problem into a definite question; (3) the postulation of a tentative hypothesis; (4) the rehearsal in the imagination of various avenues of solution; and (5) the testing of the hypothesis by overt or imaginative action (Dewey, 1916, pp. 41–53).

Dewey's five steps are employed as guidelines for students when performing their field observations and subsequent analysis in the classroom. The activity is divided into three stages: (1) observation of a fieldstone and teaching Dewey's five steps, or what is commonly known as the scientific method; (2) students select their own carved stones; and (3) analysis of an entire family plot. Although the discovery of unusual stones generates a lot of enthusiasm, this activity can be adapted for students not able to access an actual site by using slides, photographs, or a series of grave rubbings.

Stage 1

Armed with notebooks, measuring tapes, and cameras, the class proceeds to the oldest section of the cemetery. It is preferable to locate headstones made from fieldstones that do not bear any inscriptions. Once the initial excitement has abated and students are seated around the stones, the following question is asked. What can one learn about the early social life of this community from these early grave markers? Quite often the response is, "Nothing, these are just old rocks, what can we learn from them?" Through direct observation and some gentle prodding, students begin to talk about what they observe. They discuss the size of the stones, material, shape, and placement. It is essential that they conduct their own observations. After a list is compiled, they formulate a number of tentative hypotheses. Several examples follow:

1. The use of old rocks rather than carved slate might mean that the early settlers were poor, illiterate, or running from hostile Indians.

2. The short distance between the head and foot stones seems to indicate that people were shorter than today or that this might be a burial ground for children.
3. All the stones are placed in the same direction, which might reveal something about their religious beliefs.

The student's list provides a basis for additional questions. Through the use of Dewey's method, a crude profile of early life in the colonies emerges. This profile is confirmed or rejected in the subsequent classroom discussion following the completion of the field experience.

Stage 2

Dewey's method is reinforced throughout Stage 1 so that, at its conclusion, students are ready to select their own gravestone and present some tentative hypotheses regarding the history of the departed individual whom they selected. Their analysis is presented with a photograph or grave rubbing upon completion of this activity in the formal classroom. Soon, they discover patterns that offer clues to their past. Twenty to thirty grave rubbings and photographs displayed in the classroom create a visual impact that gives students an appreciation of their own town's history.

Inscriptions on the stones contain enough information for students to derive explanations almost immediately. It is the task of the student to use this information to develop a hypothesis that more fully explains the circumstances surrounding the death. The following two epitaphs are taken from student-selected stones.

Sheridan
Son of
Jonathan Philbrick, Esq.
& Sarah His Wife
Was Instantly Killed
by Lightening, While
at School
June 30, 1824
Aged 11 years

* * *

Otis S.
Son of
Langdon & Elizabeth S.
Brown
Died Dec. 25, 1848
Aged 9 Mos.

Readers may draw their own tentative hypothesis that might explain the events surrounding the deaths of these two young people. These epitaphs easily transcend the social science curriculum and can be incorporated into writing and science activities. With a degree of historical insight and imagination, short stories can be written to help students think about history in a way that connects them to it. High levels of infant mortality suggest areas of investigation in health, nutrition, and fertility patterns of the earliest settlers.

Stage 3

By this time, students are not only excited by their own investigations, but they also possess a sufficient degree of expertise in order to analyze an entire family plot, with the expectation that they will write a generational history. Here, the students trace births, marriages, deaths, and events over time. From the individual study in Stage 1 to the generational analysis in Stage 3, patterns are more clearly defined, and tentative explanations suggested in previous stages can be confirmed or rejected.

When all three stages are completed, a new world has opened to the students. Through their own observations and research, they have learned about some of the lives of our country's earliest settlers. They can make generalizations as to infant mortality rates, multiple marriages, occupations, ethnicity, levels of wealth, and changing religious and social attitudes. In a sense, they have written their own history.

Expanded Curriculum and Conclusion

The value of this activity is that students are involved in a problematic situation, one that requires active participation. Gravestone analysis in a field setting also provides opportunities to expand the curriculum in a variety of ways.

1. *Specific disciplines within the social sciences.* Demographic patterns can reveal population trends and patterns of ethnic diversity, which can be compared to regional and national movements. Students interested in economic issues can discern shifts as evidenced by type and quality of stones. Religious and social attitudinal changes have occurred several times in our history and are manifested in gravestone inscriptions.
2. *Interdisciplinary investigations.* Science and social studies offer exciting possibilities to study the reasons for infant mortality and, conversely, longevity. Disease and epidemics can be investigated in terms of health and sanitation knowledge. The cyclical nature of fertility patterns prior to 1750 offers puzzles for the inquiring mind. Language arts can be employed to teach basic writing skills, to understand poetry and imagery among the earliest citizens, and to introduce literature written during

that time. Writing a social history of a family based on gravestone analysis combines historical research and imagination, the kind of data historical novels are based on. No study of cemeteries is complete without an understanding of the art forms employed by the carvers. An investigation of medieval and Renaissance art is crucial to understanding the art forms inscribed on the earliest stones.

Dewey best sums it up when he states that "the inclination to learn from life itself (or in this case death), and to make conditions of life such that all will learn in the process is the finest product of schooling" (Dewey, 1916, pp. 41–53).

Reference

Dewey, John. (1916). *Democracy and Education* (reprinted 1961). New York: Macmillan.

Additional Readings

Dewey, John. (1902). *The Child and the Curriculum*. Chicago: University of Chicago Press.

Duval, Francis, and Ivan Rigby. (1978). *Early American Gravestone Art in Photographs*. New York: Dover.

Gillon, Esmund Vincent, Jr. (1966). *Early New England Gravestone Rubbings*. New York: Dover.

Ludwig, Allen I. (1966). *Graven Image: New England Stone Carving and Its Symbols, 1650–1815*. Middleton, CT: Wesleyan University Press.

READING THE NEWSPAPER

Effective citizenship demands an awareness of the current issues that affect our lives. Probably no source other than the local newspaper can provide the most up-to-date information, analysis, and opinion regarding the burning issues of the day. As a "living social studies textbook" (Guenther, 1986, p. 3), it is a supplement to the materials used in the classroom. The value of using newspapers for middle-level students is that they can connect local issues that have a great impact on them to global issues that may seem remote but, in fact, are not. As a vehicle for effective citizenship education the newspaper offers a host of curriculum possibilities. The following list supports the argument that newspapers ought to be used in conjunction with other curriculum materials.

1. First and foremost, the newspaper provides a real-life referent for the teaching of social studies concepts and skills; that is, initial learning, retention, and transfer are increased if students perceive a connection between the classroom and the world of everyday life.
2. Although this is an overly simplified statement, it is believed that motivation is a key to learning, and relevance is a major key to motivation. A focus on current and perennial issues and problems, with the newspaper as a resource, is viewed as real and, thus, relevant to students.
3. The newspaper is an adult medium and will become the social studies textbook for the majority of adults.
4. The newspaper is a continuous written record of our lives and times. It is one of the basic data sources for citizenship participation.
5. The newspaper itself is an influential part of our democracy and deserves to be studied as part of a total social studies program.
6. The newspaper is local and, as such, relates information and events directly to the lives of all students. It is, in effect, a microcosm of our lives and times.
7. The newspaper overcomes textbook lag and bridges the inevitable gap between where the textbook leaves off and the existing world begins.
8. The newspaper, depending on how it is used, encourages student activity and involvement and engages the student directly in the learning process.
9. If used wisely, the newspaper will develop in students a desire to read and the skills necessary to read critically and reflectively. (Guenther, 1986, p. 3)

The newspaper provides the information to pursue a problem-solving activity. Neustadt and May (1986) present the following guidelines in attempting to understand a problem:

The first is the Goldberg Rule. With some definitions of concerns in hand ask, "What's the story?" How did these concerns develop?

The second device is timelines: Start the story as far back as it properly goes and plot key trends while also entertaining key events, especially big changes. Don't foreshorten the history in ways that may distort it.

The third device is asking journalist's questions: As the timeline answers "when" and "what" don't omit to ask also "where," "who," "how," and "why." (pp. 235–236)

Once students have defined the problem as it is now, they are in a position to propose a series of tentative solutions, of course, always subject to revision. In fact, the newspaper is the starting point from which to analyze the history of the situation or issue, describe the current reality, and propose solutions. Using the five themes, the following activities will enable teachers to create stimulating classes that not only engage the students but also, more important, develop the skills to become effective and responsible citizens.

The following activities were selected from *Using The Newspaper in Secondary Social Studies* by John Guenther (1986), presented as an educational service of *The Milwaukee Journal/Milwaukee Sentinel.*

Location

Determine the distance between and location of cities in the news. Use a world map to indicate distance and location. Indicate, by using headlines, why the cities are in the news. How long would it take to travel from city to city using various modes of transportation? If only one person or a few people are involved with events in different cities, you could indicate their itinerary and travel time. If you were able to visit places in the news, where would you go? What schedule would you follow? What problems might you encounter? What places would you avoid? Why? What is the climate like in various cities in the news?

Using date lines, locate cities, states, and nations that are currently in the news. Calculate distances from your own community.

Using a map, locate the major physical features of the earth that are in the newspaper.

Collect stories about tornadoes, earthquakes, floods, and blizzards, and show where they occurred on a map.

Determine the latitude and longitude of cities and nations that are in the newspaper.

Keep a record of the temperature in some important cities in the world. Note the latitudes and compare with other cities in the United States.

Use newspaper articles to learn cardinal directions.

Some places make headlines every day. Other places might make it once every year. In a week's time, identify the most remote or unusual date line. Locate the date line on a map.

Use a newspaper map to compare a section of a city or state with an actual road map of the same section.

Show newspaper photographs of various locations and identify the location at which the photograph could have been taken. Give reasons for selections.

Read news stories that show how location affects the progress of a city or a nation. Point out the importance of climate, waterways, and terrain, especially in regard to the U.S. position as a world power.

Provide a newspaper and a time zone map. Select an event that has or will occur at least 1,000 miles away. Determine the local time at which the event occurred or will occur.

Use travel ads from the newspaper to stimulate interest in other countries. Locate cities and countries, and determine travel routes, tourist sights, major cities, and so on.

Compile a list of geography terms that are found in the newspaper that would help to describe a geographic point. Determine the factors for the location and growth of selected cities and future growth patterns by collecting and reading photographs and articles on land development, taxes, new businesses and industries, and population trends. Determine the geographical factors that are influencing these growth patterns.

Place

Post a large world map on a bulletin board. Clip and post headlines and stories referring to specific places. Keep a map of the world in a notebook. When news of a country is reported, place the name of the country in the notebook and color that country. See if it is possible to gather news from all countries on one continent. Use news stories to teach new words related to geography, such as *delta, monsoon, panhandle, harbor,* and *terrain.* Discuss the way the words are used in newspaper stories. Over a period of time, cut out newspaper photographs of climates, topographies, and natural resources, and describe the characteristics of each. Prepare a booklet on the physical features of a state, using pictures and articles from newspapers.

Create a weather center in your room with just an empty bulletin board and a student-drawn map of the United States and some cardboard weather symbols similar to the ones used on television weather reports. Each day, give the weather report based on information reported in the daily newspaper. How does weather in various parts of the country affect our local weather?

Clip out newspaper stories about the physical makeup of our planet, classifying them under such headings as water, soil, climate, topography, atmosphere, and resources.

During holidays look for articles that deal with foreign customs and traditions on similar holidays. Compare why the holidays originated in each country and how they are celebrated today.

Select a topic, place, event, or person that is of historical interest to you and is of significance to the history of your community. Research your choice, and write a feature story about it. You may want to read a couple of feature stories to help you with the writing style. If relevant, consider interviewing community members about the topic of your story. Include illustrations if they apply.

Distribute a variety of maps from the newspaper that are different in scale of miles. Rank the maps from the smallest scale to the largest. Finally, identify any large-scale maps that fall within the area represented on the small-scale maps. To show the difference between the viewpoint of a journalist and that of a historian, write a news story describing a historical event as if you were a journalist living at the time of the event. Write a historical account of a current event. Today's news is tomorrow's history. The newspaper provides us with a chronicle of important daily events. In the future, some of the events will be considered important, and others will be considered of little consequence. The historian decides what is and is not important. Assume that you are going to write a history book of your community from its beginnings to the present day. Examine your newspaper for a period of 1 week or so. Is there any news about your community that you are likely to include in your history book? Identify the stories, and indicate why you would include the information in your book. Because space in your book will be limited, you must be selective. Collect background information about people in the community from the obituaries, and write biographic articles about them. Read the editorials related to your community for a period of 1 week (or longer if possible). Identify the topics that are discussed in the editorials. List the topics on a sheet of paper and briefly describe the writer's point of view. Also, indicate whether you agree or disagree with what is said. How do the topics of the editorials relate, if at all, to community news stories?

Select at least five stories originating in your community. Rather than writing a full article describing the national importance of one story, write a sentence or two about the national importance of each of your choices. People contribute to community life individually and in groups. Most communities have numerous organizations that are designed to contribute both to the welfare of their members and to the community in general. Read the newspaper for a couple of days, and list the different community organizations that are mentioned. Describe, as near as you can tell from what is included in the newspaper, the purpose of each organization. Indicate your personal view of the value of such organizations to life in your community. You may need to do some additional research.

Every community has problems of one kind or another. The problems may be the same or different from those in other communities. The problems may be old or new, serious or seemingly insignificant. After reading the newspaper for a few days, identify ten problems facing your community. List them on a sheet of paper and rank them in order of importance. Identify the problems that you believe are unique to your community.

It is impossible, of course, to know for sure what our economy will be like in the year 2000 A.D. Each of us may, however, have our own projections of community life in the not-so-distant future. Assume that you are reading your community newspaper in the year 2000 A.D. Hypothesize about what might be included as "news" on the front page. You do not need to limit yourself to only local news. List at least six headlines that might appear, along with the lead paragraph of each news story that would accompany the headline.

Region

What geographical areas are reported in the news? Does the news differ from one geographical area to the next? What events are reported? What events continually appear in the newspaper from the different areas of the world or nation? Develop a world map to show countries in the news for a 1-week period. Prepare a bulletin board to report your findings. Compare the results of this activity completed a few weeks later.

Choose a specific region to study, and make a product map of that area. Cut out advertisements of the products and paste them on the map.

Obtain papers from other regions of the country, and compare and contrast the kinds of information, opinions, and attitudes that appear in them, with those of a local newspaper. Point out differences caused by geography. (The same activity could be done with countries.)

Over a period of time, collect pictures and articles of world cultures. List those qualities that are basic to all cultures and those qualities that are not. Identify factors that affect the development of cultures, such as advertising, religion, sports, communications, and travel. Speculate on the future development of world cultures and whether they will become more similar or different. Develop crossword puzzles on a region of the country or some other nation. Include facts that relate to the climate, population, products, major cities, historic spots, water industry, and resources.

Human–Environment Interaction

Use a weather map for map-reading skills. Identify states and cities, and discuss how the weather of that area will affect the industry and economy of the area.

Find pictures and articles about the history of an important city. Assume the role of an early settler in the city, and describe the changes that have taken place since you first settled there.

Using a newspaper and a history book, compare the problems and risks of the early explorers with the explorers of space today. Use pictures and articles from the newspaper that reflect people's basic survival needs in the modern-day world, and then compare those needs with those of people during the different ages of history. Discuss the similar and different methods people have used to meet their basic needs. The early settlers were a strong group to withstand the hardships of settling a new land. List some of the characteristics they might have had. In the newspaper, find people of today with similar characteristics.

Collect articles related to humankind's progress. What new discoveries, inventions, or products are reported in the paper? Compare articles of the same type from papers 10, 20, or 30 years ago. What stories indicate people's attempts to deal with progress? Predict articles related to progress that may appear in future papers.

Movement

Divide the class into four groups. One group will be responsible for drawing a wall-size map of the U.S. The other three groups will be responsible for following the major basketball, football, hockey, and baseball teams. Have the students make symbols for each team, and attach the symbols to the map in each team's hometown position. As the teams move around the country for competitions, students can move the team markers.

To improve map skills and stimulate interest in current events, follow the route of a government official as he or she travels throughout the country or around the world. Show the route taken on a map with colored yarn or a marking pencil.

Plan a vacation. Use the travel section and various ads for information regarding transportation and lodging costs, history of the area, points of interest, climate, and appropriate clothing. Locate the route and destination on a map. Prepare an imaginary trip around the world to a number of different countries. Write newspaper articles about places visited.

Determine the importance the Bill of Rights has played in past and present history. Research the meaning the amendments had for our ancestors. Discuss the meaning of the amendments today. Do some research to discover what events have changed the Bill of Rights' original meaning.

Determine the part the free press has played in the history of our democracy by researching how freedom of speech and the press influenced past events and are influencing current events. When the Declaration of Independence was written, a list of complaints against England were included. Find news stories in which Americans are protesting today, and compare them with the Declaration of Independence. During election campaigns, bring in clippings of speeches by candidates and articles that outline party platforms and discuss important issues. Then compare actions by political parties with those of earlier days.

To show that history tends to repeat itself, locate current events that appear to repeat events of history in terms of background and outcome. Make a table of correlations between current events and historical events. For example, immigration to the New World versus displaced persons or refugees.

Encourage students to watch the newspaper for significant statements made by prominent persons that might become famous quotations in the future. Place these quotations on the bulletin board, and discuss the circumstances around which the statement was made.

Collect pictures and articles about present-day reformers and the problems they are attempting to correct. Then, study the reformers of our past and compare their problems and tactics with those of today.

Identify the major concerns that run through our nation's history. Some of these concepts would be: labor versus management; civil rights and liberties versus state and social welfare preservation; radical dissent versus social and political consensus; ruralism versus urbanism; federalism versus states rights; foreign involvement versus isolationism; realism versus idealism in foreign policy; minority versus majority rights; violence versus law and order; and conservation versus development. Look through newspapers to find articles related to these concepts. Trace their development through history, and then discuss how it could change and what new directions it could take in the future.

References

Guenther, John. (1986). *Using the Newspaper in Secondary Social Studies*. Milwaukee, WI: The Milwaukee Journal/Milwaukee Sentinel.

Neustadt, Richard E., and Ernest R. May. (1986). *Thinking in Time*. New York: The Free Press.

AUTHOR INDEX

Alexander, W., 3, 4, 6, 10, 11
Allen, J., 71
Allen, M. G., 11, 35, 39, 81
Alm, A., 139
Apple, M., 34
Atwell, N., 99

Backler, A., 134
Banks, J., 39
Barr, R., 18, 19, 20, 21, 22, 24–25, 35, 37
Barth, J., 18, 19, 20, 21, 22, 24–25, 35, 37
Bates, J., 148
Baumrind, D., 52
Beane, J., 6, 34, 50, 79
Berg, K., 163
Bettelheim, B., 149, 155
Boyer, P., 117, 118
Braddock, J., 57
Bragaw, D., 32
Breternitz, D., 82, 84
Brooks, K., 12
Brown, J., 51
Butts, R. F., 35, 37, 102

Callahan, W., 103
Carey, H., 162
Carpenter, F., 150
Cassidy, E., 31
Cerny, J., 79
Chancellier, P., 85
Chapin, J., 24

Cherryholmes, C., 104
Child, W., 67
Christensen, M., 75
Cleary, R., 104
Clegg, A., 39
Colglazier, W., 139
Commager, H. S., 22, 26, 27
Costa, A., 99
Crandall, R., 68
Crews, K., 85
Curwin, C., 33
Curwin, R., 33

Daniels, R., 22
Davis, O. L., 4, 7, 8, 9, 10
Dewey, J., 97, 108, 109, 131, 149, 165, 166
Disbrow, S., 156
Doane, G., 74, 75
Dobson, D., 30
Duckworth, E., 51

Eakle, A., 75, 79
Easley, J., 4
Edwards, F., 12
Edwards, N., 65
Eichorn, D., 46

Fitts, J., 66
Frazer, J., 126

Garvin, J., 45
George, P., 6

Georgiady, N., 45
Georgiou, C., 149, 152, 155
Gillman, A., 163
Gould, A., 48
Gouldrup, L., 79
Greensberg, J., 162
Gross, R., 24
Guenther, J., 168, 169, 170

Hallman, R., 50
Harleman, D., 131
Harmin, M., 33
Hartoonian, H. M., 32, 104
Heilbroner, R., 21, 136
Helburn, S., 4, 7, 8, 9, 10
Hepburn, M., 30
Hoffman, M., 50
Howe, L., 33
Howe, M., 33
Hullfish, H. G., 13

Inhelder, B., 50

James, J., 50
Jenkins, J., 98
Jewett, J., 65
Johnston, J. H., 7, 46
Jones, V., 75
Joyce, B., 24

Kates-Garnick, B., 139
Kirschenbaum, H., 33, 34
Kitchens, J., 27

176

SUBJECT INDEX